THE MAGNIFICENT OBSESSION

David Swartz

D1045775

NAVPRESS

A MINISTRY OF THE NAVIGATORS
P.O. BOX 6000, COLORADO SPRINGS, COLORADO 80934

The Navigators is an international Christian
organization. Jesus Christ gave His followers the
Great Commission to go and make disciples
(Matthew 28:19). The aim of The Navigators is
to help fulfill that commission by multiplying
laborers for Christ in every nation.

NavPress is the publishing ministry of The
Navigators. NavPress publications are tools to
help Christians grow. Although publications
alone cannot make disciples or change lives,
they can help believers learn biblical
discipleship, and apply what they learn to their
lives and ministries.

© 1990 by David Swartz
All rights reserved, including translation
Library of Congress Catalog Card Number:
   89-63848
ISBN 08910-92889

Cover illustration: Wendy Reis

Some of the anecdotal illustrations in this book
are true to life and are included with the
permission of the persons involved. All other
illustrations are composites of real situations,
and any resemblance to people living or dead is
coincidental.

Scripture quotations in this publication are from
the *New American Standard Bible* (NASB), © The
Lockman Foundation, 1960, 1962, 1963, 1968,
1971, 1972, 1973, 1975, 1977.

Quotation on pages 166-167 from *I Stand by the
Door* by Helen Smith Shoemaker. Copyright
© 1967 by Helen Smith Shoemaker. Reprinted
by permission of Harper & Row, Publishers, Inc.

Printed in the United States of America

Contents

For my son, Steve—

> *whose mind has eyes to*
> *see a thousand kingdoms*
> *yet unknown,*

and

For my daughter, Karen—

> *whose eyes are the windows*
> *into a heart big enough to*
> *hold a thousand kingdoms,*

> *Who both belong to the*
> *One Kingdom that will*
> *never fall.*

Author

—•—

David Swartz is pastor of Dubuque Baptist Church in Dubuque, Iowa. He has a rich background serving in college campus ministry, street ministry, church outreach, and pastoral work. He received a B.S. from Clarion State College and an M.R.E. from Southern Baptist Theological Seminary.

Dave is the author of *Dancing with Broken Bones* (NavPress). He and his wife, Gay, have two children, Steve and Karen.

Acknowledgments

I believe only madness, conceit, or incompetence could lead a writer to think he could produce a book all by himself. Hoping to declare myself as free as possible from all three, I wish to openly express my gratitude. I thank Gay, my wife, without whom any and all ventures in my life would seem somewhat hollow. Her encouragement in so many ways made this happen. I thank my kids, Steve and Karen, about whom the dedication of this book says it all.

I want to thank all those who have allowed me to tell their stories. While their names have been changed in this book, they are recorded accurately and indelibly in the Book of Life.

Donna Monthey and the print room staff of the University of Dubuque Theological Seminary did generous and fast work in duplicating the manuscript.

It is a deep honor to have my name appear above that of NavPress—to be a partaker and beneficiary of their Christ-centered passion for excellence. Professionally and in ministry, the whole gang is without peer.

I especially acknowledge the grace of God as administered through the red pen of my editor, Jon Stine. Having collaborated on two books together, I have found him to be an insightful critic, teacher, and encourager, iron that sharpens my iron, friend and brother in Christ. He's a consummate professional who can hear a book banging around inside a writer and knows how to shake it out. As he embodies much of what I wrote, I thought of him often during this process. I stand much in his debt; he stands in my mind and heart as a good soldier of Christ.

A woman once said to me,
"Dr. Jones, you are obsessed
with the kingdom of God."
I wish that were true
because that would be
a magnificent obsession.
—E. Stanley Jones

1
A Kingdom of Fire

The kingdom of God is God's redemptive love, righteous justice, and shining holiness pressed into every facet and dimension of human endeavor. God desires to rule over all He has created, to rule in the hearts of men and women. Jesus Christ said that His followers were to work and strive to advance God's kingdom above all else. Even if this means squeezing out the last drop of our sweat, blood, energy, time, and substance, this desire to advance God's kingdom is to be the consuming passion of every Christian: "Seek *first* God's kingdom."

The first Christians understood the primacy of the Lord's calling. They left home, family, and careers without regret. They challenged both civil and religious authorities when necessary. Torture and death brought praises of Christ to their lips. Today we have more difficulty understanding this kind of commitment.

People don't seem to understand what the kingdom of God is all about. The church of Jesus Christ, once born in fire, is now encased in ice. The passionate zeal that inflames genuine seekers of God's kingdom is rare. Today self-interest seems to eclipse the biblical call to self-sacrifice.

Zealots of a dozen or more ambitious causes run off in as many directions crying, "This is the way! Walk ye in it!" The resulting chaos and ambiguity of purpose leave many sincere Christians wondering if anybody really knows what the church should be about. And what in the world is the kingdom of God?

Our society, which once looked to Christ's church for direction in every field of endeavor, now considers the church unnecessary. The world that is supposed to be salted with God's people has become increasingly hostile and indifferent to any public statements the church makes. The world regards us as a relic from another time. Perhaps it is our attempt to straddle two different kingdoms that destroys our capacity to prophetically and redemptively address our culture for Christ.

As Christians we have one life to live. Will it be lived encased in ice—safe, but dead? If we will leave the comfort and convenience zones of our lives for the single searing flame of the pursuit of God's kingdom, we can begin living on the cutting edge of a life that will be risky and even dangerous. But those who have committed to the fire instead of the ice will tell you that the flame does not consume them but transforms them into the very likeness of Jesus Christ. Theirs is a life of depth and power. People like these transform the world around them.

To claim to know Jesus Christ and yet to be a stranger to this life of total commitment is a tragedy and a waste. So is the spiritual death of people and nations around us. The times demand decision.

So we must ask ourselves some important questions about the large picture. What *is* the kingdom of God? Is it relevant to our lives today? What implications does it have for the world? What should it mean to me personally?

If you have never clearly understood either what the kingdom of God is or what it means to put its pursuit above everything else, read on, with a willingness to go through the fire of commitment.

THE KINGDOM OF THE KING

In the eyes of His contemporaries, Jesus failed. He had many opportunities to consolidate the masses who had been drawn into a "movement." That's certainly what many expected. But Jesus avoided mobilizing the masses into a quasi-political faction or a revolutionary force bent on military takeover.

The crowd's subsequent disillusionment with Jesus explains their unhealthy vacillation—praising Him as the Messiah on Sunday and then screaming for His blood on the following Friday. At the cross, only a handful remained out of what was once thousands. Yes, to the naked eye Jesus tragically wasted the opportunity to build a physical kingdom for Himself, and thus paid with His physical life.

But Jesus hadn't come to set up an earthly, physical kingdom to rival men like Herod or even Caesar. Just as we do today, the people then were always trying to squeeze Jesus into the mold of their wants and expectations. In His mind and in His words, Jesus was clear: the kingdom of God is not a geopolitical entity. No one can trace its boundaries on the pages of a Rand McNally. No one can enter it by having a properly stamped passport or by registering their goods at customs. King Jesus said as much in John 18:36: "My kingdom is not of this world. If My kingdom were of this world, then My servants would be fighting. . . . My kingdom is not of this realm."

What is the kingdom of God (or the kingdom of heaven, as it is sometimes called)? Since Jesus Christ said it was the one thing we should pursue at all costs, we should *strive* to know what He meant. But how can we seek something we can't completely define or understand? Working through things like this sometimes sparks conflict, but we must do it. There are some Christians who claim to have trouble understanding theology but are just too intellectually lazy to think deeply. For people called to love God with all their mind (Matthew 22:37, Mark 12:30, Luke 10:27), refusing to think is sin. Faith is no exemption clause from utilizing the muscles of thought.

The Bible portrays God as being a king—and not just one king among many but as one over all. But He is not a passive king sitting on a throne to be fawned over by self-seeking subjects; He is a King on conquest. He is a Creator whose creation has turned against Him. The roots of rebellion go back to pre-Eden when some of God's own angels defied Him in a grab for power and position. Defeated and banished from heaven, these rebels chose earth, not as a second front for another assault but as a theater of revenge.

The third chapter of Genesis has implications that transcend space and time. God created man, loved him, and gave him authority over everything on earth (Genesis 1:26-30). Then, when Satan enticed man to disobey God, man became subject to the whims and machinations of evil forces, the chains of his own sinful nature, and the repercussions of living in a world bearing scars of a chaos it never wanted. As man's authority suddenly evaporated, Satan scurried to establish a kingdom of his own—a rebellion state, a stolen throne, usurped authority. In spite of the brilliance of technology and the explosion of our cumulative knowledge, humanity and the cosmos are lying in the grip of a supernatural evil tyranny: "We know that . . . the whole world lies in the power of the evil one" (1 John 5:19).

Any earthly king facing an insurrection of this magnitude and having the power to smash it would do so, probably with a ruthlessness matching the venom of the rebellion. And make no mistake: God has the power. The sheer power that resonates throughout the pages of Scripture erupts unpredictably in awesome and even frightening ways. If it were a matter of sheer force, not only would God have vindicated Himself long ago but evil and suffering wouldn't have extended down to the present day. Why does God delay?

Again, as Jesus said, the kingdom of God isn't the retaking of geopolitical or even cosmic real estate. The reign and throne God wants most of all are those in men's hearts. Jesus said, "The kingdom of God is not coming with signs to be observed; nor will they say, 'Look, here it is!' or, 'There it is!' For behold, the kingdom of God is in your midst" (Luke 17:20-21).

We've handled the most profound reality in the universe with such familiarity and indulgence as to render it bland and dull. What is it? *The love of God.* The sheer might that could vaporize Satanic forces at will could also overpower and override the negatively charged particles of a person's soul, compelling him to repent and believe. But that would be coercion of the human psyche. God has volitionally limited His power by choosing to desire a love relationship with man. In this kind of relationship, neither side can be forced. Deep love is a primary part of God's nature that is difficult for us to fathom. People who've seen it clearly have always abandoned questions because of their awe and worship. "Neither death, nor life, nor angels, nor principalities, nor things present, nor things to come, nor powers, nor height, nor depth, nor any other created thing, shall be able to separate us from the love of God, which is in Christ Jesus our Lord" (Romans 8:38-39).

God delays restoring His kingdom because He is waiting for His family to be completed. As God's children, we become impatient. The evil and suffering around us are great, and we want it to end. It would be so much better to enjoy God's presence directly, to see Him on His throne.

Why can't God just hurry up the process? Why does He allow the sin and pain to go on and on? Well, although He is grieved about all the evil and suffering, God is confident in His sovereignty and power. He will eventually not only crush evil but completely eradicate suffering, with all its scarring effects.

God knows as a wise Father that our love for Him has given us tunnel vision. We can see at times only our desire to be with Him, despite the fact that there are untold millions yet to become His children. He not only wants us to be patient, but He wants us to join Him in the quest for one more find, one more heart.

God has a far broader perspective than we do. He's not cornered in by space and time: "With the Lord one day is as a thousand years, and a thousand years as one day. The Lord is not slow about His promise, as some count slowness, but is patient toward you, not wishing for any to perish but for all to come to repentance" (2 Peter 3:8-9).

But God's kingdom is more than just individuals coming back under His reign through Jesus Christ. As God lives through His people, some of that spiritual life rubs off in a collective sense. The institutions, structures, and cultures true believers inhabit are permeated with God's grace, righteousness, and justice. The kingdom of God is a spiritual salvation that inevitably impacts daily life and society. People who are brought into the kingdom of God through Jesus Christ live differently. They can't rest until their families, neighborhoods, communities, and nation order themselves in alignment with God's kingdom.

Jesus Christ Himself will indeed return to set up His

kingdom, which will supersede all earthly governments. But until then, Christians in every age and every culture are the seed of a whole new age. As the people of God, it is not our function to chisel new boundaries from established borders, air space, and territorial waters. Rather, it is our calling to dissolve the self-interest, greed, and hatred that stand behind all the disputes over real estate and other material wealth.

ANOTHER CULTURE, ANOTHER PLANET

Friends of ours have relatives serving in the diplomatic corps. Preparing for a new assignment in Pakistan, the couple plunged into an intense crash course on the culture. Why? Obviously because they can't spend the next three years hidden away in the embassy compound. Entering another culture can seem like landing on another planet. One major reason we have difficulty understanding Jesus' preoccupation with the kingdom of God is that we read the Bible through Western eyes. Almost two thousand years and a formidable cultural rift separate us from the life and times of Jesus.

Jesus lived in an age when everyone knew what a monarchy was, the authority inherent to the throne, and the respect and obedience due it. Going back centuries before Rome, all the nations of that part of the world were monarchies. Some still are. Everyone knew his own role. The king was not just a figurehead but the one who decreed national policy. The people were subjects who followed policy. When Jesus spoke of the kingdom of God (or, synonymously, the kingdom of heaven), His words were addressed to minds who already grasped the basic concepts rooted in that culture.

Modern Western society, especially the United States,

works out of a cultural grid that fogs understanding of the kingdom of God. Our revolutionary beginnings and democratic form of government obstruct rather than help us. Our history resounds with the battle cry of a people who have repeatedly proven that they'll fight fiercely for the freedom to govern themselves.

Our democratic form of government places supreme power in the hands of the people. We're used to making our opinions known and we expect our leaders to listen and to implement wherever they can. An elected official who merely dictated policy to his constituents would be out of work by the next election. We put them in office and pay them. They should serve us and not vice versa.

To complicate things, some of our constitutional fruit has gone bad. Some good things provided for in founding documents or once embraced by societal consensus have either been eroded or selfishly redefined. We no longer venerate our leaders. Because of public scandal and general cynicism, political leaders at all levels are subjected to both mistrust and open disrespect.

Some important words have been redefined in ways that could contribute significantly to the collapse of Western culture. We've taken words like *liberty* and *freedom* and stretched them to the breaking point. Originally these words included the necessity of restraint found in civil law at all levels and the willingness of the individual to sacrifice for the public good. But today freedom rarely means more than the absence of restraint, internal or external.

Morally, freedom has decayed into license. As long as we don't murder or rape (or at least don't get caught), we demand the freedom to do whatever we please. We resent much of the restraint of civil law we do have. And if our wants and interests aren't met soon enough, we clothe our agenda as an issue of human rights.

Since these issues have now become issues of human "rights" instead of mere autonomous desires, no one should deny them to us. We will have them regardless of how many legitimate rights of others are trodden underfoot in the process.

There is little willingness to sacrifice for the public good. The top priority is "number one"—*self*-interests. Our rights, our wants, our agenda.

In view of all this cultural baggage, it's no surprise that we Americans have trouble grasping Jesus' idea of the kingdom of God. Almost everything in our history and culture is geared to avoid it.

RESISTANCE—IT'S PERSONAL

The problem of not understanding the kingdom of God runs deeper than history and culture. It also has spiritual roots. As Paul points out, "The god of this world has blinded the minds of the unbelieving, that they might not see the light of the gospel of the glory of Christ" (2 Corinthians 4:4). A satanic strategy of obscuring the truth of Jesus Christ is presently at work throughout the world. Whenever spiritual growth stagnates, our appetite for the truth wanes, sinking into spiritual darkness. The uncomfortable fact is that we are not helpless victims of this fallen culture or of spiritual warfare; we are *accomplices*. We can't point all our fingers outward. At our core we understand the kingdom of God well enough to feel the threat of its absolute claims.

Our sinful nature is far more robust than we care to admit. Cultural and psychological masks serve as only a thin disguise. Underneath we have a strong resistance to being told what to do by anyone—including God.

Samuel Brengle was a pastor who lived in the late nineteenth century. He was enthralled at what God was doing through William Booth and a motley bunch of fire-brands called the Salvation Army. Resigning his large church, Brengle went to England to join up with Booth. He sensed immediately that Booth wasn't thrilled to have such a "successful" man join him. Somehow Brengle didn't fit in. His involvement was jerky and stiff, out of synchronization with the effective ministry of others who were neither as learned nor as experienced.

Discouraged, on the verge of quitting, Brengle went to Booth and laid bare his heart. Fastening Brengle with a piercing gaze, William Booth said, "Your problem is that you've been your own boss for too long."

Samuel Brengle is not alone. The kingdom of God and Jesus' claims to be Lord of that kingdom challenge our self-supremacy. We intuitively perceive Jesus' claims of kingship or lordship as a primary threat to our desire to fully control our own lives. The government and our bosses may tell us what to do. Our families may make demands we acquiesce to. But deep down in our heart is an area we clutch feverishly, where *we* control, *we* decide, *we* rule. When Jesus Christ approaches the throne of every human heart He always finds it filled by someone who would almost rather die than vacate. We've been our own bosses too long to bow graciously to another King and to submit to His kingdom.

Does Jesus really lay this deep claim on every life? Viewed through the lenses of what Western Christianity has become, you wouldn't think so—not if what we see around us is normative. But Jesus' absolute claim to rule over the hearts of men was part of things from the beginning. He commonly allowed others to address Him as "Lord"—a word meaning master and a covenant title in the Old Testament for God. He taught that obedience was the only proper response to His demanding teaching—not negotiation or a dash for the commentaries to get a second opinion. His command—"Follow Me"—challenged people to abandon their most cherished dreams for the sake of His kingdom. And He really expected them to make that commitment. Those who did sounded the same note to others with gusto.

Jesus Christ was, is, and always will be a Savior who forgives sin freely and demands total commitment in return. Looking at what Jesus gives in return, we know that it isn't too much to ask. He no longer approaches men as an itinerant carpenter, but as a King on conquest. Looking across both centuries and galaxies, His purpose is to transform not only individual lives but whole cultures, and even physical creation itself. For all of us who've heard His voice and claim His name, Jesus' conquest of a runaway planet should be our main business.

In a society where tolerance stretched to its breaking point is seen as a virtue, we must choose. Uncomfortably, Christ presents only two alternatives. If we're not for Him and His kingdom with all our heart, soul, and mind, then we are against Him. If we shy away from true commitment, if we don the shabby rags of religious games and pretense, then we are rebels. And while faithful subjects may expect to enjoy the good graces of their king, a rebel faces only one end: banishment from the kingdom.

The good news is that the One who could command angels recruits from His enemies. All of us were enemies, but if we accept a commission in His conquering kingdom, we are His subjects and His friends. We are committed to pursue His kingdom as people who recognize the vitality and value of its refining fire.

2
The Invitation

It was a rainy night. I received a phone call from a friend who desperately wanted to talk. He said he was scared. We agreed to meet at a coffee shop. As I splashed down the sidewalk to where the flashing neon threw orange reflections into the street, I wondered what I was getting into.

My friend was waiting with the latest stroke of adversity to his complex story of lamentations. A doctor said that he needed knee surgery. Even if the operation succeeded, he might not walk again.

But there was so much more to the story. He had been through his share of trials. First, he suffered birth defects—a borderline retardation that specialists said would eventually render him unable to walk or talk. There had been open-heart surgery at the age of twelve. He'd been shot, stabbed, suffered from epilepsy, fathered a birth-defective son, and had his face burned away in a fire. Now facing the possibility of spending the rest of his life as an invalid, he said to me, "I'm not sure I have anything left to face this."

My friend didn't know it then, but he stood on the edge of a momentous opportunity. It's not just people looking

toward major surgery that wonder what's left. People cling-
ing to deteriorating marriages or suffering in the wake of
the psychological amputation of divorce wonder the same
thing. So do highly successful career people dismissed
without notice because of a merger or cutback.

When life undercuts our competence, comfort, or
security, we're in a great position to hear God's voice as He
calls us to a new life focus: His kingdom. God knows our
fickle, vacillating hearts well. His offer of redemption and
His kingdom confronts boldly every person on two broad
fronts and compels, even demands, that we choose.

PLEASE HAVE ME EXCUSED!

Jesus confronts us in two parables with a grand invitation.
He tells of two nobles who planned great feasts, one a
wedding and the other occasion not stated (Matthew
22:1-14, Luke 14:15-24). The second feast may have been
out of the sheer generosity of the rich man's heart. In both
cases, these were real bashes with all the stops pulled out.
But while it may have been a slight not to be invited, for
some of the people it was definitely an inconvenience to go.

Weddings and catered feasts are great occasions. They
fill many of our June weekends with fun and excitement.
And usually, to not go—even if it's not our first inclination—
would offend the family. In these parables, to refuse an
invitation from an oriental noble was a serious insult. But it
was done with cavalier flair, indifference, and lame excuses.
(Making an investment purchase, operating a business, and
daily personal relationships were all more pressing.)

Many of us have truly important things that need
attending to. Maybe there's a new house or a new job.
Maybe we're newly married or emotionally involved or
sexually entangled. Perhaps we need to finish school.

There always seems to be something.

In these parables things didn't stop with mere excuses. The servants bringing the invitation were met with hostility and anger. Maybe those invited sensed how threadbare their excuses seemed. When the last sophisticated evasion falls flat, violence can result amid the frustration and embarrassment. Certainly such hostility fell to Jesus, who was shockingly despised and rejected by men (Isaiah 53:3). The apostles were hounded from city to city suffering violence and abuse. The early church lived through the shell-shock of a series of persecutions at the hands of Roman emperors who were either masters of political expedience or utterly demented.

Christians still make strong enemies. The twentieth century has seen more blood spilled for Jesus Christ than any other. Right now Christians suffer slander, political pressure, sanctions, separation from families, physical abuse, torture, and death. Our relative ignorance, prayer-lessness, and inactivity in the face of these spiritual attacks does not become us. In a television dramatization, the Apostle Peter learns that many Christians, including Paul, have died in persecutions in Rome. With his voice trembling, he says, "God forbid that this should be going on and that I should not be part of it." Well said—particularly in light of the biblical call to pray for those in prison as if we were in prison ourselves (Hebrews 13:3).

So, those who were invited to the feasts rejected the offer. Did the nobles tell the violinists to pack up and send the caterers away? No, they did something amazing. They invited the outcasts, people who never would have been invited anywhere—the poor, lame, and blind. Street people! Imagine them gingerly inching their way into the courtyard, staring in disbelief and awe, afraid to touch anything.

The kingdom of God offers an incredible invitation to

enter where we don't deserve to be invited. When we approach the Cross, we enter into the presence of God. This sense of unworthy awe is a good sign that we have our spiritual wits about us.

This invitation isn't for somebody else, for someone who "obviously" needs it. Sin is the cancer eating away at us all. Someone suggested to me that the average person tells over three hundred lies a day. At first I was skeptical. Then I wondered who we'd be telling all these lies to. Now I know. Although they may not total three hundred, we do a lot of lying to ourselves. Many Christians live as if they're almost too decent to need a Savior. Living like that, we lie to ourselves.

Our worship has built-in reminders of our need for God's invitation. Six times a year I stand behind a table where silver trays are filled with bread and grape juice. Before we break bread and share the cup, we stop to remind ourselves that the poor, blind, lame, and crippled are still invited to the King's banquet table. To come to that table thinking any other way of ourselves paints a picture not of a man gone blind but of a skull without eyes.

The invitation to the kingdom of God isn't grand just because it cleanses sin-crippled people and enables them to leave all their sin behind. It calls and spurs people on to become what is humanly impossible to achieve.

When we enter the kingdom, we become part of a family that has God as its Father. Paul wrote, "You have not received a spirit of slavery leading to fear again, but you have received a spirit of adoption as sons by which we cry out, 'Abba! Father!'" (Romans 8:15-16, Galatians 4:6).

The homeless waifs of old London were a constant backdrop throughout the pages of Charles Dickens—a poignant vestige of a hard, though quaint, time. But for people like William Booth, who saw those children staggering in gin-induced stupors, dying of exposure and starvation, being hung for petty crimes, they were a heartrending reminder that God's kingdom invites men to call Him Father—and that He's capable of living up to all that name means, even if an earthly father isn't.

"People seldom nod off during the reading of a will." Charles Spurgeon was right. When there's something in it (whatever "it" is) for us, we're all eyes and ears. The words of Paul should snap us to attention as he continues, "And if children, heirs also, heirs of God and fellow heirs with Christ" (Romans 8:17). The invitation to join the kingdom of God in Jesus Christ is grand also because it extends an offer to receive an inheritance that is indestructible and utterly undeserved.

"Fellow heirs with Christ." What does He have as an inheritance? Pictures almost too profound to be slipcovered in words flood the mind—glory, majesty, throne. All these are to be Christ's, and ours as well! What more ennobling things could someone receive? If it weren't for two more facets of the grand invitation, we could stop here easily believing this to be too good to be true.

Not only does God adopt us into His family and make us fellow heirs with His Son; He commissions us as His ambassadors, His personal envoys, to the world: "We are ambassadors for Christ, as though God were entreating through us; we beg you on behalf of Christ, be reconciled to God" (2 Corinthians 5:20).

A friend of mine travels all over the United States and Canada for his company, which markets construction equipment. In every way he's expected to give a good representation. Foreign ambassadors are also carefully chosen and prepared. But unlike the polished and often pampered envoys of today, God's blind, lame, poor, and crippled ambassadors don't always get the red carpet treatment. They must remember who they are and give a good representation.

E. Stanley Jones tells this story:

> I arrived one day at Pahleve, Persia, which is now Iran, on the shores of the Caspian Sea, to go up to the capital, Teheran. The man in charge of transportation had difficulty because there were more passengers than cars. I saw a car with only one passenger in it, so I said to the man in charge, "Why can't I go in that car? There's only one man in it."
>
> He said, "I'll see." But he came back crestfallen and he said, "I'm sorry, sir, but the man said you couldn't ride with him because he is a French diplomat and you are only a missionary."
>
> I suppose I should have felt squelched, but inwardly I straightened up and I said to myself, "If he is a French diplomat, then he represents a shaky French kingdom, which has had twenty-six governments in thirty years. I am an ambassador of the unshakable kingdom of God, which has had one government since the foundation of the world and will have one government to the end."
>
> Later, on the way across the Caspian Sea by boat, the diplomat got caught by a treacherous lock in the men's room and couldn't get out. He waved at me frantically and he said, "Please sir, extricate me!" So the ambassador of the kingdom of God extricated the diplomat from France.
>
> Is that what the ambassadors of the kingdom must do—extricate the diplomats of the world who have boxed themselves up in impossible ways of life? If they only knew it, they are crying out in more ways than one, "Please, sirs, extricate us." And we must

humbly but assuredly say, "Brother, this is the way. Walk in it, the way of God's kingdom."[1]

Jesus also invites us to enter the kingdom of God to become His friends. Real friends are comparatively rare. Sometimes one comes along who is genuinely noteworthy. As a college student, I had the opportunity to work with the vice president of the school. He's retired now and a building on campus is named after him. For some reason I'll never understand, he chose to befriend me.

He would "shoot" at me under the table with his pipe while attorneys poring over legal documents made long meetings even longer. A secretary held his calls while he told me about seafood restaurants in Boston. I was only a student with no claim on him, but he extended his friendship as a gift I'll always treasure.

Jesus said, "No longer do I call you slaves, for the slave does not know what his master is doing; but I have called you friends, for all things that I have heard from My Father I have made known to you" (John 15:15). Jesus Christ does more than desire us as friends; He prizes us as a treasured part of His inheritance (Ephesians 1:18). To esteem this rare privilege lightly shows that we don't really know Jesus Christ, that we're blind to the cosmic loneliness in our own soul that cries out for Him.

Jesus issues the invitations to the kingdom in earnest; they're written in His blood. We're compelled to take His invitation seriously. Just as it's dangerous to reject the invitation of an earthly king, how much more a heavenly one?

THE DARK SIDE OF THE KINGDOM

The second broad front of the kingdom of God is that it demands an account of all who reject it. Judgment isn't a popular subject, but we can't escape it. It's actually woven into the fabric of human existence. In spite of situational ethicists and values clarification people, a fundamental sense of rightness and wrongness permeates much of man's dealings. We're still capable of outrage. We're incensed when innocent people are victimized in self-centered lawsuits or when criminals go unpunished. We cry out that things aren't fair and should be set right. Is God blind to this or out of touch with what's going on? Jesus has wisdom for us:

> He presented another parable to them, saying, "The kingdom of heaven may be compared to a man who sowed good seed in his field. But while men were sleeping, his enemy came and sowed tares also among the wheat, and went away. But when the wheat sprang up and bore grain, then the tares became evident also. And the slaves of the landowner came and said to him, 'Sir, did you not sow good seed in your field? How then does it have tares?'
>
> "And he said to them 'An enemy has done this!' And the slaves said to him, 'Do you want us, then, to go and gather them up?'
>
> "But he said, 'No; lest while you are gathering up the tares, you may root up the wheat with them. Allow both to grow together until the harvest; and in the time of the harvest I will say to the reapers, "First gather up the tares and bind them in bundles to burn them up; but gather the wheat into my barn."'"
> (Matthew 13:24-30)

Jesus is saying that until He returns, the world will be a cauldron where good and evil intermingle. Isn't that true? Isn't it the way things have always been? Look at history and the evening news. Don't monsters like Hitler and Stalin (not to mention lesser monsters we've known personally) seem to have escaped the justice that was their due? Haven't decent people suffered needlessly and without relief?

Look at the Bible. Aren't even the most devout people nothing more than a carnal mixture of the same emotions, drives, and mixed motives that keep all of us tripping over our own clay feet? The good and evil grow up together in the world and in our hearts. But the sorting process of the two is surely coming: "It is appointed for men to die once and after this comes judgment" (Hebrews 9:27).

Since we all must face such a solemn occasion, does anyone have an edge or the inside track? All of us know good people; most of us *are* good people. Surely, in facing God, good people like us will come out on the right side.

The air above the street shimmers with the July heat and every step poofs up small dust clouds that cake on shoes and socks. In weather like this I down ice water in large glasses. But if you brought me a tall frosty glass of iced tea, and parenthetically mentioned that there were three drops of arsenic trichloride in it, I'd leave it alone. It's only three drops, but three drops of something poisonous.

We normally tend to view our sin as through the wrong end of the looking glass, miniaturizing it. What we see as trivial, as a quirk, God sees as high crimes against Himself. No matter how good we may be, there's always enough sin to render us guilty.

When humanity is divided between the wheat and the tares as Jesus described, being "religious" won't have an edge. Attending church services or having religious beliefs won't be enough. Vladimir Ilyich Lenin, the architect of modern Communism, admired Jesus profoundly. He even memorized the four gospels—but without life-changing results. Jesus put this kind of religious attitude in perspective:

"Not everyone who says to Me, 'Lord, Lord,' will enter the kingdom of heaven; but he who does the will of My Father who is in heaven. Many will say to Me on that day, 'Lord, Lord, did we not prophesy in Your name, and in Your name cast out demons, and in Your name perform many miracles?' And then I will declare to them, 'I never knew you; depart from Me, you who practice lawlessness.'" (Matthew 7:21-23)

Has anyone held expectations over your head that you absolutely knew you couldn't meet—maybe on the job or in a relationship? It's suffocating and crushing to try and yet never measure up. God expects men to keep His Law, and yet the best of us—religious or not—have fallen short. In brilliant style, Paul makes the point regarding man's facility for "measuring up": "All have sinned and fall short of the glory of God, being justified as a gift by His grace through the redemption which is in Christ Jesus" (Romans 3:23-24).

You know those lies we tell ourselves? One is that after death we're all going to the same place. But Jesus has indicated that we are *not* all going to the same place. The idea of judgment and hell are certainly fearful and repulsive to us. The only thing that forces me to believe in them is that the statements of their malignant, threatening reality fall from the lips of Jesus Himself. How could we ever be free to elevate our opinion above His?

We're standing on serious ground. The New Age craze and the secular drift of society have functionally reduced Jesus Christ to a spiritual equivalent of "Mr. Potato Head"— the popular toy with a featureless head that can be made up to look any way we'd like. We deify our own beliefs and then expect Christ to conform. And in the process we tell ourselves another one of those lies, one that starts out saying, "God, to me, is . . . ." A dean of Oxford once said that if God exists, it doesn't matter at all what we think of Him but rather what He thinks of us.[2]

Whatever you or I think, God is under no obligation to conform to our opinions; He is who He is. He is the God who said, "I AM WHO I AM" (Exodus 3:14). And He's revealed to us what He's like in His living Message, His Word—Jesus Christ (John 1:18). We have no right to put Him through the blender of our self-centered viewpoint or to change the flavor of His teaching by mixing it with ancient Egyptian occultism or Eastern mysticism. God is out to reclaim a wayward humanity. The reign of the kingdom He has in mind is over hearts just like ours.

> There was something about the crucifixion that made every witness either step toward it or away from it. . . .
> And today . . . the same is true. . . . It's the Continental Divide. It's Normandy. And you are on one side or the other. A choice is demanded . . . the one thing we can't do is walk away in neutral. No fence sitting is permitted. The cross, in its absurd splendor, doesn't allow that. That is one luxury that God, in His awful mercy, doesn't permit. On which side are you?[3]

If we are not surrendered to Jesus Christ and His kingdom with all that we are, then we are against Him—no matter how good, moral, or religious we may be. Now He stands before us extending the incredible invitation to come to Him as Savior and Lord. Even if we have fallen into sin or we're playing religious games, the invitation is still extended. We must take Christ for all that He is and nothing less. The feast is spread and the invitation, a lifetime lottery-winning opportunity, has been sent. But remember, invited guests have neither the right nor the authority to edit or rewrite the terms of the invitation.

3

A Revolutionary Movement

———◆———

Our kids were starting to get nervous. We were taking them down a deserted alley just like the ones we've told them a thousand times to avoid. Passing dusty warehouses and deserted loading docks, we entered a door marked with a weathered bronze sign. As the door closed behind us, we found ourselves in the receiving room of a rather outdated shipping company.

In the dim light I saw a lever protruding from the wall; I pushed it. Immediately the sound of machinery began to grind deep inside the wall. The bookshelves of elegant leather-bound volumes that filled one wall smoothly slid away to reveal a hidden passageway. We stuck our noses in, then stepped just inside. The second we did so, the wall slid shut. There was no lever on the inside to open it. I know, I looked.

Squinting through an atmosphere of deep purple light, we groped along the wall and felt the passageway veer to the right. As our eyes adjusted to the darkness, we could see clearly where we were going—nowhere! A wall loomed up out of the shadowy corridor, leaving us wondering what was next. We reached out tenuously to touch the wall. It slid away. All at once we heard a voice coming from the darkness: "How many in your party, sir?"

We guardedly stepped into the cryptic spy-motif restaurant, a veritable museum of espionage gear with a décor straight out of Paris, Tangiers, or Casablanca. But this was only Milwaukee.

Make no mistake about it: Everyone who comes by faith to Jesus Christ enters the most revolutionary enterprise a human being can undertake—a pursuit of the kingdom of God. Christ always enlists people to a conspiracy—a cause so radical and so rarely popular that in its purest form it must often go underground. Under the guise of old First Church on the corner, an inner-city mission in a run-down store front, or a beehive of ministry encased in the massive stone and glass walls of a thousand-member congregation, Christianity only appears to be harmless and safe. It's actually a well-run conspiracy under the able steerage of God, who integrates even the tactics of the enemy into His strategies (Acts 4:27-28).

In a tight conspiracy, everyone involved in the network knows the code words and countersigns, the objectives and strategies. Christians are to be no exception. Jesus laid down lines of operation for the kingdom of God. He did so not merely to satisfy our curiosity as to how the kingdom operates but so that, in our dim moments when we become dull or enshrouded by circumstances, we will not abort the cause and, by so doing, become its enemy.

YOU CAN'T KEEP GOD'S KINGDOM DOWN

Five wads of dough sit in a plastic freezer tray. They don't look like much, but what a full night in a bread pan and forty-five minutes in an oven can do! The yeast expands the dough and the oven browns and bakes it into fresh bread that we devour with thick butter slabs.

With His eye on the yeast, Jesus said, "The kingdom of heaven is like leaven, which a woman took, and hid in three pecks of meal, until it was all leavened" (Matthew 13:33, Luke 13:21). Leaven is the same as yeast. Symbolically, leaven in Scripture represents influence that begins embryonically but then grows until it has full control. The influence may be positive (as here) or negative (Matthew 16:12, Mark 8:15, 1 Corinthians 5:6-8, Galatians 5:9). Although only a small quantity is normally used, the final effect of the leaven is nevertheless complete.

Jesus taught that implicit within the kingdom of God is a restless tendency to expand its influence. Spiritual yeast. It seems to have a life of its own, never resting in the quest to deepen, heighten, widen. Its tendency is to saturate lives, communities, nations, and society with the transforming nature of Jesus Christ.

One evidence of this kind of yeast is that when people attack Christianity in order to silence or exterminate it, they only serve to spur it on. Men like Peter, John, Paul, and Silas were thrown into jail, then sprung by angels or freed by a conveniently timed earthquake. Shabbily clothed Christians in prison today testify to being bathed in mysterious warmth while being held in ice covered cells. The death of men like Stephen culminates in the conversion of men like Saul of Tarsus. The deaths of missionaries, instead of scaring people away from the missions enterprise, send our finest young people stampeding to give their hearts and lives to that same cause.

How can we account for this kind of metamorphosis on a human level? We cannot. But something drives and compels millions to press on relentlessly when everything human in them cries out to quit. What is it? The indwelling life of Jesus Christ presses on. The leaven never rests until the entire loaf is saturated.

But Jesus' parable says nothing about how fast this is supposed to happen. Sometimes the kingdom surges ahead as people come to Christ in droves, with waves of reform changing society. Sometimes it slows to less than a crawl as a dead, apathetic, often wealthy church gives the lie to what Christ and His kingdom are all about.

G.K. Chesterton wryly remarked, "At a number of times in its history, the church absolutely went to the dogs. And in each instance it was the dogs that died!" Out of the most barren graveyard of the church, the working leaven of the kingdom of God is agitating to bring life.

Sometimes that's hard to believe. I went through some angry days as a young Christian. At my college, things were booming. People were finding Christ, their lives being changed and redirected. Christianity was being integrated with and expressed through every academic discipline and artistic medium. But this was on campus. I saw next to nothing going on in the church, and so I self-righteously concluded that if God was going to do anything in the world He would have to use college groups like mine. I could see leaven only when it was at work on my own kind of bread.

But God showed me a different way of leavening. He used a short, stooped, bespectacled man named Howard Blanchard to open my eyes. Howard pastored the church closest to campus, the one many of us attended. He deeply wanted to see something jell spiritually with that congregation. Because of church politics, Howard had been hurt, frustrated, and discouraged many times. While the controlling group wanted respectability, Howard had set his heart on the kingdom.

Although he never saw much in the way of tangible results, Howard never quit, became bitter, or felt his church owed him success. He was too busy being leaven and leaving the results to God. Over the course of time, God used people like Howard to melt my heart for the church. It's as if He was saying to me, "Dave, it's My church, not yours. Why don't you let Me decide when it's useless and dead? You just be leaven."

Are you concerned about your church or fellowship? How deeply? Are you merely upset that they don't offer the ministries and services you'd like? Or do you grieve over the contrast between what Scripture says and what you see on Sunday? Your grieving and heart sickness may earmark you as God's leaven. The easy thing would be to bail out and leave where you are. And indeed the time may come for that. But, for now, think of doing something revolutionary: Don't leave. Stay and be leaven. It may get tough. You may find yourself a minority (even a persecuted one at that) but then most conspiracies are, aren't they?

ALL THAT FROM NOTHING

Ice from a vicious winter storm has paralyzed the area. But spring is coming. The first seed catalog arrived just before Christmas with its vividly colored promises of mammoth tomatoes and maximum yield on strawberries. Seeds are singularly unimpressive things—hard little nuggets often resembling gravel. But the marvelous fragrances and flavor those seeds eventually produce send us digging into the March soil.

Jesus found a picture of a second operative principle of the kingdom of God in a strange place—a small seed: "The kingdom of heaven is like a mustard seed, which a man took and sowed in his field; and this is smaller than all other seeds; but when it is full grown, it is larger than the garden plants, and becomes a tree, so that the birds of the air come and nest in its branches" (Matthew 13:31-32).

We live in times when many of us know how to get things done in this technological world, how to build a successful business venture and how to put a career idea into action. Any entrepreneur worth his Rolex knows that fledgling enterprises must begin with polish and class. If a consulting firm had been contracted to plot the launching of the kingdom of God, all the trappings would have been in place.

At a press conference, the chairman of the board introduces the CEO, a man carefully screened and chosen from thousands of applicants. After laying out confident success scenarios in their opening remarks, these two then guide the media people into a catered reception in the office suite—premium space in a major office complex. Blueprints, they assure us, are already underway for a complex of their own. From eye-catching logos emblazoning the walls to state-of-the-art communication systems and technology, everything is "uptown."

But the kingdom of God is, in utter contrast, a conspiracy of sorts. Conspiracies have small beginnings, small like a mustard seed. When God entered our world, what was He like? How would most of us visualize Jesus? Well, He was born to a woman who, although pregnant, still claimed her virginity. Raised in a small town of low regard (John 1:46), Jesus spent thirty years with people who saw Him every day without noticing anything that set Him apart as *deity* (Matthew 13:54-58). His only admission of being a king fell from His bruised and bleeding lips when He stood before Pontius Pilate (John 18:33-37). His life was cut off in the most painful, disgraceful way a society of that day could engineer.

The model extends to Christ's followers. Would you launch a worldwide venture with the people Jesus chose? The disciples were shot through with more than enough fatal flaws to sink the whole cause. Their only qualification was that they had been with Jesus (Acts 4:13).

Through the course of time the pattern hasn't changed. An obscure monk named Luther suffered anguish of soul that intensified until the explosion of the Protestant Reformation rocked Europe. William Carey, the father of modern missions, was a poor cobbler who couldn't find an audience among churchmen for his notion that God wanted His people to reach the many overseas who'd never heard the name of Jesus. The well-known evangelist D.L. Moody had been a shoe salesman in Chicago.

God does not care at all whether or not we are eminently qualified; He only desires that we be eminently available. His confidence lies not in our pedigree but in His Spirit and His grace:

> For consider your calling, brethren, that there were not many wise according to the flesh, not many mighty, not many noble; but God has chosen the foolish things of the world to shame the wise, and God has chosen the weak things of the world to shame the things which are strong, and the base things of the world and the despised, God has chosen, the things that are not, that He might nullify the things that are, that no man should boast before God. (1 Corinthians 1:26-29)

The college campus I mentioned earlier was swept along by the Jesus Movement of the late sixties and early seventies. Two small Bible studies mushroomed into a movement of over two hundred people. And what a mix of backgrounds and theology. We didn't realize how little we knew. We were bold in Christ and we loved each other. Today I wince to remember some of the things we said and did. But great things happened for the kingdom of God. He sent people from that campus around the world. We were idealistic and foolish enough to believe God wanted to use us to change the world. As we stay in touch after all these years, we're still idealistic enough to believe it.

Some friends of mine in a nearby town run a Christian bookstore. If you catch the wife in an unguarded moment she'll say candidly that she doesn't want to be doing this. She wants to be what she was before—a nurse, and a very good one. But coming to Christ a few years ago out of a difficult emotional past, she left nursing and opened this store with her husband. You should see it—window displays and décor of true quality, with innovative display and floor use. People often say it's the most beautiful store they've ever seen.

On top of this, the store is a center of ministry as Christians from the area meet to share and pray with each other in the aisles. These two are doing consultant work with stores all over the country and soon will be video-taping. Nursing was great, but she tended to rely on herself and her own resources in that profession. But now she and her husband are thrust into a new spot in life where they can't touch bottom, and they must trust Christ all the way. And great things for the kingdom of God are occurring.

Recently I heard a church choir from a nearby city. Their singing throbbed with the joy and pathos found only in black gospel music. More than once my cheeks ran with tears of joy as I saw and felt the gospel bubbling out and swaying back and forth in our choir loft. But this wasn't just a choir; they were friends. And that, too, brought tears.

Drugs, domestic violence, and so much other heartbreak have wounded many of these people. But here they stood, singing so enthusiastically that their praises to God literally shook the building and led one of our little ones in the nursery to ask her mother if she and Daddy had been upstairs dancing to a rock band! These folks have sung in maximum security prisons, witnessing hard, bitter men melted to meekness.

The joy of this choir is no narcotic; it's evidence that God's Spirit in the human heart is the medicine that heals sorrow and pain and changes lives. That's revolutionary! Their qualifications? They're merely foolish things to confound the wise. And they love it so!

God has exciting plans for everyone who sets out on the quest for the kingdom of God. He wants to use all of us to genuinely bless people throughout the earth. Jesus taught that when the mustard plant was fully grown, all the birds of the air could nest in its branches. God's vision is always global in scope. Our vision tends to be narrow and myopic, but He has all the nations in view. As His commission to His followers, Jesus said, "Go therefore and make disciples of all nations, baptizing them in the name of the Father and the Son and the Holy Spirit" (Matthew 28:19).

While other faiths have definite ties to culture, Christianity has rooted well around the globe. Our provinciality, ignorance, and spiritual conceit steer us into seeing Christianity as a uniquely Western possession. It is not.

> Christianity has been the means of reducing more languages to writing than have all other factors combined. It has created more schools, more theories of education and more systems than has any other one force. More than any other power in history it has impelled men to fight suffering . . . from disease, war or natural disasters. It has built thousands of hospitals, inspired the emergence of nursing and medical professions and furthered movements for public health and the relief and prevention of famine . . .

men and women awakened by Christianity brought
about the abolition of Negro slavery and wrote into
the laws of Spain and Portugal provisions to alleviate
the ruthless exploitation of the Indians of the New
World . . . from no other source have there come as
many and as strong movements to eliminate or regu-
late war and to ease the suffering brought about by
war. By its name and symbol the most extensive
organization ever created for the relief of suffering
caused by war, the Red Cross, bears witness to its
Christian origin. The list might go on indefinitely . . .
ideals in government, the reform of prisons and
emergence of criminology, great art and architecture,
and outstanding literature.[1]

FOR OPEN EARS ONLY

My phone rang. On the other end was a young woman, a
new Christian. I could hear the confused irritation in her
voice: "Why did Jesus heal people and then tell them to
keep quiet about it? Why did He intentionally say things in
such a way that people would not understand?" She was
asking questions about a third operative strategy of the
kingdom of God. It comes as a mystery.

And He was saying to them, "To you has been given
the mystery of the kingdom of God; but those who are
outside get everything in parables, in order that while
seeing, they may see and not perceive; and while
hearing, they may hear and not understand lest they
return and be forgiven." (Mark 4:11-12)

Jesus wasn't shutting off everyone from repentance by
speaking cryptically or unintelligibly. He wasn't echoing the

sentiments of the prophet Jonah who absolutely refused to go to Nineveh because someone might actually listen and repent. There's something deeper here. In the Bible, mystery refers to "the secret thoughts, plans and dispensations of God which are hidden from . . . human reason, as well as from all other comprehension below the divine level, and . . . must be revealed to those for whom they are intended."[2]

This may help us understand the idea of mystery, but it doesn't clear up the biblical situation. Is Jesus really withholding truth from desperately seeking people? Maybe you've listened to a citizen's band (CB) radio. Its users have a language all their own. No one can listen for long without hearing someone squawk through static, "Hey there, good buddy, got your ears on?" Jesus asked people the same thing in His own way. At least sixteen times He is quoted as saying, "If any man has ears to hear, let him hear."

Jesus was here expressing a primary concern: whether or not those who heard Him were predisposed to take what He said to heart. The inclination to love, serve, and worship God enhances understanding, our ability to "hear"; the inclination to love, serve, and worship self erodes it. Jesus said, "If any man is willing to do [the Father's] will, he shall know of the teaching, whether it is of God, or whether I speak from Myself" (John 7:17).

The parables of Jesus are like a litmus test that measures either the acidity or basic content of the soul. Those who understood gave evidence of a genuine hunger for God that was present already. Those who didn't, either got over their spiritual ambivalence quickly (since the foundational matters of their own lives lay in other directions) or they hated Jesus because He spoke of them in unflattering ways. Their loss of face overrode any concern for the truth. Anyone genuinely seeking spiritual truth will never find Jesus obscuring it.

When Jesus came preaching to His hometown, He was repudiated (Matthew 13:54-58, Mark 6:1-6). These people had watched Him grow up, seeing Him every day of His life. That was the problem. They'd bottled and labeled the Son of God like a specimen in a biology lab. Wasn't Jesus the son of the people down the street? Didn't He and His brothers and sisters play in the street every day? But when Jesus confronted them as One who explodes all categories, they bristled. Who does this guy think He is, saying all these things?

The people who should have known the Lord Jesus best showed that they didn't want to be jarred from a private self-centered womb paneled with feeble dreams and furnished with the urgent concerns of this world. Even Jesus seemed astonished at their unwillingness to have "ears to hear."

Before the temptation to be smug becomes too strong, remember that we're all very much like these people, and there's little room for denial. We want compartmentalized beliefs that readily identify heretics and provide ammunition against cultists and the junk music our kids listen to. But do we want a Jesus who doesn't hesitate to demolish some of our most cherished and ingrained values, showing them to be either reinforced prejudice or mere window dressing? Unless God shouts audibly from the sky, we assume that He's committed to the same old status quo, including all the trappings, that we are.

These people in the town where Jesus grew up show how dangerous it is to be willfully blind to truth that is readily available. A spiritually deaf man can know volumes of truth and heed nothing. A man who can hear the mysteries of the kingdom of God will make any sacrifice necessary to walk in the light of even the tiniest shred of light he possesses.

THE DIVINE ROMANCE

A fishing boat trawled past the harbor mouth with no intention of turning in. But within minutes, a bizarre compulsion seized the entire crew of rough fishermen and so the boat docked in the harbor. The men were obsessed with their sin and what would happen to their souls if they died. They combed the town going from door-to-door until they found someone to tell them of Christ.

What caused this strange compulsion to come on them in the first place? No sermons had been preached and they were far away from religious men. The harbor town was clenched in the jaws of God in spiritual awakening. The presence of the Holy Spirit was so intense that even fishermen sailing by fell under His power.

As we seek His kingdom, we find God almost always doing something different from what we would expect. Although He never violates His Word, He constantly reminds us that "as the heavens are higher than the earth, so are My ways higher than your ways" (Isaiah 55:9). This unexpectedness of His hand is another strategy of the kingdom that could be called the adventure-loving nature of God.

Sometimes it's absolutely thrilling. Many people laugh at the disciples' reaction at seeing the risen Jesus. But we'd have done the same. Dead people stay dead! What a spiritual checkmate Jesus' resurrection was, what a coup for the kingdom of God!

Other instances come to mind as well. The Apostle Paul was prepared to launch into an unreached area named Bithynia. It seemed like a natural; many are the mission boards who would see the hand of God in it. But the Holy Spirit blocked Paul repeatedly, ping-ponging him across Asia Minor until, at an Adriatic seaport, Paul stood poised to launch the evangelization of Europe.

Some church growth experts estimate that the average person comes to Christ after at least five exposures to the gospel. But no computer can project how penetratingly God can confront people from countless directions, in countless ways. People feel strange urges to pray, only to learn later of how real needs were met. Preachers have the strong compulsion to speak a message that later bears magnificent fruit that could not have been anticipated. The adventure-loving nature of God can be thrilling.

Sometimes we become confused about what's going on in the spiritual realm. Some of us who've studied or read a few books posture as if we've grasped all biblical truth—we have God all figured out. God is locked into the multi-colored prophecy chart in the back of our Bible. He stopped doing certain things after the apostles died or after all the books of the New Testament were written.

Peter Lord wryly notes, "We have some charismatics who think God should heal everyone. And we have some Baptists who think God doesn't heal anymore. So you know what God does? He lets a charismatic die and heals a Baptist in spite of himself just to show He's God and no one's going to tell Him what to do." Beliefs we passionately held and even fought for will be found to be incorrect. Part of our spiritual growth inevitably includes intellectual repentance. We'll fiercely believe things only to find that we were wrong. We must either change or fossilize.

Second, we will also see God use people we've ruled out of the kingdom or have given up on. Joe was a mess—a Christian, but still a mess. He was still banging his head repeatedly on the same things. We were always covering the same ground. He'd drop out of sight for several weeks only to pop up again back at square one. Finally he disappeared totally. I heard he was going to another church. One day my phone rang and one of our members said, "Guess who's coming over?"

"Who?" I said.

"Joe!"

"Oh." I tried to sound enthusiastic but didn't pull it off. I thought, *Oh, no! Here we go again!* But boy, was I wrong. Joe had straightened out. All his bills and fines were paid. His wife had become a Christian and they were piecing their marriage and family back together. Joe had even been invited before a panel of judges and police officials to give advice on dealing with drugs in our area. And now he was calling this family in our church to thank them for not giving up on him. He didn't call me. I don't think he feels I gave up on him, but I know I did. Shameful egg drips from my face as I watch God, who wasn't limited by my unbelief, raise up this man in ways I hadn't even dreamed of.

God also uses people who don't match our theology stripe for stripe. Can God actually use charismatics, dispensationalists, Calvinists, Arminians, and all kinds of other believers who differ from each other on peripheral points of truth? You wouldn't think so to listen to many people carp and carve on one another. As long as the basic truths of Christianity are in place, we'd be wise to be gracious to each other.

In the heat of their ministry, George Whitefield and John Wesley came to differ over the doctrine of predestination. But they were quite gracious to each other, which is more than can be said for their followers. One abusive Calvinist asked Whitefield if he thought they'd see Wesley in heaven. "I fear not," Whitefield replied. "He will be so near the throne, and we shall be at such a distance, that we shall hardly get a sight of him."[3]

A third canvas for this adventure, this unpredictability of God, comes in the seeking of guidance. You'd think that as we mature in Christ, wrestling with guidance would get easier. Not so. We need to heed the message of Hudson Taylor. "In his younger days, things used to come so clearly, so quickly to him. 'But,' he said, 'now as I have gone on, and God has used me more and more, I seem often to be like a man going along in a fog. I do not know what to do.'"[4]

Some of the cockiest among us who seem always to know God's mind may be destined to break up on their own presumption and pride.

> Among the seven deadly sins . . . was sloth—a state of hard bitten, joyless apathy of spirit. There is a lot of it around today in Christian circles; the symptoms are personal spiritual inertia combined with critical cynicism about the churches and . . . resentment of other Christians' initiative and enterprise. Behind this . . . lies the wounded pride of one who thought he knew all about the ways of God . . . and then was made to learn through bitter and bewildering experience that he didn't.[5]

Often when we look at suffering and affliction, we fail to see reason, pattern, or sense. The strategies of God's kingdom will take a lifetime to learn and to live out. We'll have many failures and bruises of heart. But something marvelous will come, too. We'll be bound more tightly to the Lord, trusting Him more deeply. Remember, people don't join revolutions to get all their personal questions answered, but to throw their lives into the cause. We'll become liberated from the dull addiction to self to join the grandest, most adventuresome conspiracy of all time. Instead of stealing and hoarding secrets on shadowy street corners, we will shout the open secret of the kingdom of God—Jesus Christ—from the rooftops.

4
Monitoring the Heart

⸻

I awoke from a deep sleep feeling strangely as if I was suspended in midair. A nurse was holding me up off the bed while another quickly retaped the suction disks to my chest. In the hospital for unidentified chest pains, I'd been hooked up to a heart monitor. The green blips on the screen at their desk had suddenly flattened out to a straight line. And now in the middle of the night the nurses stood ready to do whatever was necessary to bring life back to that flat green line on the screen—and to my heart. Thankfully it was only the green light that went flat, which was corrected by a bit of adhesive tape.

When the pulse scanner goes straight on a heart monitor it might be nothing—maybe something as insignificant as a chest sensor coming loose. But it might also signal that cardiac arrest has choked off the pulse and that emergency treatment is needed. It's worth checking to find out for sure. In my case I'm sure glad the nurses came to find out what was wrong even if it cost me a night's sleep. So it is with Jesus' message of the kingdom of God. Jesus loves us too much to allow us to walk away from Him without monitoring the state of our heart. His message of God's kingdom demands a response and by that response, all men everywhere lay bare some of the deepest recesses of their heart.

While Jesus never needed help or advice in discerning what was in people's hearts (John 2:24-25), we do. He constructed a grid to help us develop that kind of discernment in His parable of four soils in Mark 4:1-9.

WHEN GOD'S VOICE IS CUT SHORT

First, Jesus described seed scattered along the roadside where it never had a chance to germinate because birds ate it (Mark 4:4). In His interpretation (4:13-20), Jesus showed that Satan steals the Word of God from people's hearts before it can take root.

A local college interviewed me for an article in the college magazine on the broad topic of "the future." As we sat in a coffee shop, I fielded questions about why I thought Jesus Christ made a difference in individual lives, particularly in light of the seemingly unsolvable problems in the world. I also probed a little into the reporter's hopes and dreams for the future. At one point she cut me off. "But wait," she pressed. "How can someone really have what Christ offers?" As her defenses dropped, she turned from a reporter into a seeker. Tears welled up in her eyes and hung from her lashes.

But the glint was gone in seconds. As she regained her composure and put her professional mask back in place, I saw only the glitter of big city lights and big city dreams, with no room for Jesus. It happened so quickly—the opening was there for only a minute!

That same kind of quenched tears has shown up in other places, too. On Sundays I've seen them as people leave the worship service. Sometime during the service God dents the armor of someone's complacency, raises the curtain of someone's blindness, or wounds someone's heart over sin. And the tears come. But what happens next?

Thousands of Christians whose church experience is lackluster don't know what to do when God's Spirit grips their attention. And so they do nothing. Churches are filled with people whose spiritual lives are as shallow as those of newborn Christians, even though they've walked in Christ for years. Their faith has a bland sameness to it, punctuated by occasional stirrings of insight now lost and feelings now grown cold. We leave the church and stand in groups in the parking lot frittering away in trivial conversations the deep impressions made by the Spirit of God.

Those tears, prompted by God Himself, are designed to compel us to draw aside for solitude with Him. God wants to get our attention in the service in order to continue the dialogue later. But both the tears and the opportunity to hear God's voice in a deeper way get choked off in the parking lot. Life-changing, kingdom-charged impressions evaporate amid chatter about football games and restaurants.

We come away poorer from all this than if God had never spoken to us at all. When God's voice is not heeded, when we allow it to fall into silence, a deadness or vacuum remains, along with a residual film of guilt. Satan has snatched away the seed. It's a form of self-evasion to say that the first three types of soil in this parable represent a nonChristian response to the gospel, and that since we are Christians they do not apply to us. Spiritual pathologies of the first three soil types crop up in Christians' lives all the time. We can pray fiercely that the seed doesn't get snatched from the hearts of others. But we must set the intensity of our resolve high so that when God speaks, we follow through without letting the seed be snatched away.

A GOOD START WITHERED AWAY

Jesus told of other seed that was planted in shallow, rocky soil. There wasn't room for solid rooting to develop. When the sun shone hot the plant withered because the tiny root filaments weren't deep enough to reach the moisture that could have saved it.

Names and faces float in my memory, but I particularly remember Tom. He attached himself to the Christians on our campus and quickly became part of things. Tom claimed to be a Christian and could make it sound convincing. He made the same zealous mistakes many new Christians do, but appeared to be running true. Then Tom hit two things that stopped him dead. One was his relationship with Sue, a girl he'd been seeing. She wasn't a Christian and they'd been sleeping together. Tom knew what Scripture said. Something had to give.

One Sunday Tom spent six hours on his knees trying to convince God to let him have Sue. Painfully Tom learned that God's "no" isn't negotiable. If it's "no" in Scripture, six hours of spiritual gymnastics and marathon praying won't change anything. No matter how we badger and beg Him for our cravings, God can never be coerced to give us anything less than His best. A second blow followed involving Tom's ego. He prided himself on being a hustler—a wheeler-dealer type—and was having understandable problems integrating this macho approach with his Christian life. When he was approached by some Christian friends about an area where he needed to repent, Tom bristled, "I can't do that. If I did confess that, I'd have nothing left to confess and I'd be perfect." Tom broke away from the Christians and spurned all their attempts to draw him back. He finally dropped out of school altogether.

Was part of Tom's problem that he'd gotten the idea

that Christianity was easy? Granted, he was unwilling to repent sexually and had a robust ego. But in talking with him before he dropped out of sight, I could sense that, in some way he couldn't quite describe, Tom felt betrayed. Too many glowing testimonies of victory that omitted struggle, too much talk about flawless spiritual disciplines that never allowed for failure and frustration, too many Christians who never seemed to sin—had all this conspired with his sin to help do Tom in?

God seems to lavish extra grace on new Christians. Like newborn babies, they need a great deal of tender care and their Father provides that kind of tender loving care, along with extra encouragement. New Christians often have voracious appetites for Scripture, experience remarkable victory over some sin and remarkable freedom from temptation over others, and know of extraordinary answers to prayer and envious success in evangelism.

It would be great on the human level to enjoy this kind of spiritual victory always. But it just doesn't happen. We need to tell these young and tender Christians to be sure to drive their roots deep—because the hot noonday sun is coming. Sin is tougher to beat than you think. Repentance is costly. Spiritual disciplines are not easy to practice. Prayer in some areas may go unanswered all our lives. Not everyone we know will be thrilled with our stand for Christ; we may inadvertently alienate people we love. And most importantly, you now have an enemy in Satan who is ruthlessly devoted to your destruction.

We must see growth from a new perspective. In Scripture, growth is never presented as an option but as a mandate: "But speaking the truth in love, we are to grow up in all aspects into Him, who is the head, even Christ" (Ephesians 4:15).

Spiritual growth is a mandate from God. To cease to

grow is to begin to die. There is nothing in Scripture licensing us to wallow in spiritual mediocrity for years. Growth may not be easy. If God were to show us in advance all the things necessary for us to grow, we'd probably opt out of the process. Growth in any area of life just doesn't happen without incredible effort.

We must strive to live by the grace that saved us. Many Christians unconsciously strive to maintain their spiritual lives on the basis of performance. But our failures in living the Christian life rise up like ghosts to haunt us through false guilt and discouragement. Yet, as always, God loves and accepts us, not because our obedience is flawless and our works up to standard, but because "the blood of Jesus . . . cleanses us from all sin" (1 John 1:7). Just as surely as the sun rises to blast down with its scorching heat, we will all need many second chances and much forgiveness.

As a young Christian, I believed in grace, but I saw it as a doctrine, not a living reality. Now that I've known Christ awhile and have logged some painful mistakes, grace is as fresh as the first breath of a spring morning. I believed in its existence then; I experience and marvel at it now.

No one grows, no one puts down roots, alone. All of us remember people in our lives who have strategically encouraged and rebuked us, listened to our doubts and struggles, and prayed both with and for us. We can't stop the sun from rising to its noontime blast. But we who are older and have grown spiritually can make some shade for the new ones who haven't yet put down roots—thus giving them more time to do just that.

SLOWLY BUT SURELY STRANGLED

Jesus goes on to describe a case where the seed germinated, put down roots, and grew. But around it were brambles, weeds, and thorns. Before long, thorn bushes drank up all the ground moisture available, entwined the plant, and choked it. This wasn't something that happened overnight but came on slowly and surely. A few verses later Jesus identifies the thorns as "the worries of the world, and the deceitfulness of riches, and the desires for other things" (Mark 4:19).

The things that numb most Christians are not the things that grab headlines—things like murder, rape, or dealing in kilos of cocaine. Many of us stand in extreme danger through our tiny capitulations here and there, giving in to culturally conditioned, socially acceptable ideas. We subtly allow daily issues and decisions to supersede our desire to put Jesus Christ and the pursuit of His kingdom first. College students face questions about who to marry and what career to pursue. People further on in life can become preoccupied with a home—buying a first one, moving up to a nicer one, or redecorating the current one. Or maybe your focus is a career. Possibly you've come far enough to own a sailboat or a weekend place on the lake. Maybe your leisure time is spent in a ceramics club or the Rotary.

All these things seem innocent, even admirable and desirable. But in the rush of everything, days slip through our fingers like sand and so does the love of Jesus Christ. It's so subtle and slow. Our intellectual beliefs usually remain intact at first. But the ready obedience that springs from love begins to wane, first in crumbs because our hearts are still tender enough to feel stings of guilt over low-grade rebellion. We know that things have slipped, but these "good things" just swallow our energy. As we persist, we anesthetize our conscience and fully devote ourselves to things rather than to the Savior who died for us.

Names come to mind of people who are more than just

old friends. We came to Christ together. We prayed for one another and stood together as we were reviled for our witness to Christ. Good times and precious tears were shared. But much more than years and miles separate us now. Vectoring away from Christ in the beginning at only a negligible angle, their separation from Him has increased exponentially over years. Whatever pulled them away doesn't matter. It was usually something decent and respectable, something that grew up like thorns to choke off the life in Christ that we once shared. What can we do to help others keep their focus and guard ourselves?

What a difference in this part of Jesus' parable a simple garden hoe could have made. Gardeners don't just plant seeds and walk away hoping to pick tomatoes or green beans in four months. They spray for bugs, and even more importantly, they spend warm summer evenings with a hoe cutting away everything that might choke the plants. The seeds in Jesus' story might have grown had someone done some cutting away. The best spiritual tool for this is a certain attitude held clearly in the forefront of our minds.

Jesus Christ could never give us anything more important (no matter how good and respectable it may be, or how badly we want it) than *Himself*, His will for our lives. He will never bless *anything* that He knows will compete for first place in our lives. Flippant rationalizations that say "Of *course* the Lord knows how I feel about Him!" should make us stop and think. That's the point. He really does know. He doesn't need our glib reassurances. He can see for Himself as He looks into our hearts to observe either our diligent care or benign neglect.

Nobody intentionally plants thorns where they intend seed to grow. It just happens, slowly and unobtrusively. Although recognizing this problem and cutting the thorns away is not easy, we must remember that Jesus Christ has invested His blood and grace. So He refuses to stand idly by as Christians sell their lives for societally respectable peanuts at the cost of sacrificing immortal treasure in the kingdom of God.

THE GOOD STUFF

Jesus' last description is of seed falling into good soil and reproducing a great harvest. One night I was introduced to members of a church planting team that would be starting a work from scratch. One man in particular caught my attention. He was a professor at a major university with an earned doctorate. He was also studying for another doctorate at a nearby seminary. When asked about why he decided to spend a summer in Iowa, the man replied, "I knew I could be doing a lot of things. I could teach summer sessions at the university, continuing to work toward tenure and advancement. I could take graduate seminars toward my doctorate. But I knew my life belonged to Jesus Christ. And when that is the case, sometimes you just have to put your personal concerns on the shelf and throw yourself into the kingdom of God." And so—with gusto—he spent the summer tramping down hot dusty sidewalks and knocking on strangers' doors to tell them about the love of Christ.

The life that is good seed, which reproduces a hundredfold, isn't a life without problems, without struggle, without sin. But such a person is absolutely clear on how to *spend* his life. Regardless of struggle, sin, and disappointment, he presses on. Winston Churchill said, "Success is never final; failure is never fatal. It is the courage to continue that counts." The courage fueled by the grace of God to pursue a kingdom tasted but not seen causes the seed to flourish in the most common life. Jesus Christ looks deeply to test the soil of everyone's soul.

5
A Privileged Life

God could certainly have established His kingdom in any way He chose. He could do it all by Himself, but He decided to use believers as bit players. Everything in the Christian life shouts of privilege. All that He gives us is undeserved—from the forgiveness of sin to eternal life, and everything in between.

The tone that rises out of the history of the first followers of Jesus is that, as a group, they were honored just to be included. It was a privilege to know, serve, and (if need be) to die for Jesus Christ. It still is.

But we live in a society that does not appreciate or esteem the idea of privilege that has any association with sacrifice. As we uncritically breathe the philosophical air of our times, our Christian walk loses its buoyant step and becomes heavy plodding.

In order to belong to the kingdom of God and seek to advance it, we must first and foremost live a life couched in privilege. Losing this perspective of God's grace will inevitably make any attempt to live for Christ an unnecessarily heavy task indeed.

THE DELIGHTS OF GOD

Being a father has definitely been a challenge. Along the way there have been some real delights. Gay and I have enjoyed the simple joys of capturing our kids in the act of growing up. These pop up in strange ways.

My son and I punch and wrestle each other for fun. One day as I walked through the living room he blind-sided me and bowled both me and a large stuffed chair completely over. At first he was afraid that I was hurt. This soon melted into fear that *he'd* be hurting after I disentangled myself from the chair. But seeing that I was neither hurt nor angry (I did initiate this little game and do perpetuate it) he walked away—but not before I saw a grin that showed he was kind of pleased with himself. He's getting big—and I'm working out!

When the Bible calls God *Father*, it is not just using a human image to illustrate part of the divine nature. Fatherhood at its best with all its attendant joys is part of the stamp of God's image on humanity. While human fathers sometimes cheat themselves of the joys of fathering through miscarriage of that role, God, as a perfect Father, takes full pleasure in relating to His children.

One of these is the sheer joy of giving. We need to mount a campaign to debunk the notion of the stinginess of God. We act as if blessings must be pried from His fingers or as if His goodness were sealed in a vault, only to be accessed by the right combination. Even our prayer language shows that we see God as being tightfisted. We talk about obstacles, barriers, unlocking, and breaking through when we consider fellowship with God.

A careful look at Scripture shows God not as a tightwad but as a Father who delights in many things. In Genesis 1:31, God surveys with great satisfaction the finished work of creation, assessing it as with the seasoned eye of the master craftsman. Although redeeming sinful men wounded the very heart of God, it does not follow that God forged the redemption of man begrudgingly: "For it was the Father's good pleasure for all the fulness to dwell in Him, and through Him to reconcile all things to Himself, having made peace through the blood of His cross; through Him, I say, whether things on earth or things in heaven" (Colossians 1:19-20).

Furthermore, God didn't need to be browbeaten into adopting these blatant sinners as His children: "He predestined us to adoption as sons through Jesus Christ to Himself, according to the kind intention of His will, to the praise of the glory of His grace, which He freely bestowed on us in the Beloved" (Ephesians 1:5-6).

God need not be extorted to reveal His plan. Through Scripture, He does so gladly: "In all wisdom and insight He made known to us the mystery of His will, according to His kind intention" (Ephesians 1:8-9).

A DELIGHT TO QUENCH FEAR

Jesus said, "Do not be afraid, little flock, for your Father has chosen gladly to give you the kingdom" (Luke 12:32). It's noteworthy that Jesus sets the giving of the kingdom in the context of fear. Fear is one of the most powerful motivations in the heart of man. Channeled properly it can be the muscle of wisdom and guardian of both body and spirit.

But Jesus spoke of the kind of fear that spurs men to betray their values and transgress the boundaries of sound thinking. He knew that fear can cause people who know God to live as if they did not. He knew that fear can become fastened like a leech on the deep need for hope and security that *everyone* has.

The seed bed for fear is wide and fertile. We fear for our health, children, and families. Whose job is really secure? Volatile world events, the shakiness of our national economy, and crime of all sorts can send us looking for a good real estate buy in the Himalayas. Even the institutional religious scene can leave us cringing in the face of massed opposition on all levels. What we don't need is someone merely telling us not to be afraid. There's so much to genuinely fear.

What we do need is someone like Jesus to tell us not to be afraid because He has something that uproots fear instead of merely sedating it. Jesus reassures us by telling us that the Father is giving us the kingdom. Accepting that gift and embracing it to our soul is an incredible tonic for fear. By doing so we shift the foundation of our security, hope, and significance to a level where not even death can touch them.

We must keep things in focus. God doesn't give us the kingdom to make our lives pain-free and problem-free, but to galvanize us for something infinitely more important.

The task itself is the greatest privilege. Jesus said a mouthful when He responded to Peter's recognition that He was "the Christ, the Son of the living God":

> "You are Peter, and upon this rock I will build My church; and the gates of Hades shall not overpower it. I will give you the keys of the kingdom of heaven; and whatever you shall bind on earth shall be bound in heaven, and whatever you shall loose on earth shall be loosed in heaven." (Matthew 16:18-19)

We've done so much theological jousting over this passage that we've missed the obvious. The astounding thing Jesus does is to put the reins of the most weighty venture mankind has ever seen into the hands of people manifestly unequal to the task.

Have you ever known someone who somehow believed in you more than you could ever believe in yourself? The unwavering confidence of Jesus Christ in the church over the centuries is staggering—and it's not because the church has earned it. He knew what a bunch of spiritual incompetents and malcontents He'd be working with. His confidence was not in them. Rather, Christ stands utterly confident in what His blood, His grace, and the Holy Spirit can accomplish—turning the humblest life into a showcase of His power.

While some tasks intimidate and belittle, having the keys of the kingdom of God in the hands of the church stretches us to live in Christ's power, up to His expectations. Listen to one man's account: "Today you will meet all kinds of unpleasant people; they will hurt you, and injure you, and insult you; but you cannot live like that; you know better, for you are a man in whom the Spirit of God dwells."[1]

The church today badly needs a renewed sense of both the privilege and the responsibility of being entrusted with the keys of the kingdom. While some of the talk from unbelievers about hypocrites in the church is rather transparent excuse-making, the criticism bears some resemblance to the truth. Even in their darkness, many people sense intuitively that the church should be living for something much higher than the sanctified navel-worshiping they too often see. These people recognize that they should be seeing something more, something higher.

Although the church will probably always have this charge of hypocrisy thrown at it, we can steal the thunder and sting from the charge by living up to the privilege of carrying the keys of the kingdom of God in an intimate relationship with Jesus Christ. Men throughout the centuries have considered it an honor to die for Christ's kingdom. We can surely do no less than to live for it.

BINDING AND LOOSING

Set in Jesus' words to Peter are two more aspects of the privilege of belonging to the kingdom. One is found in the word *loose*. What does it mean? A Christian must view life as currency not just to be spent, but to be actively invested in "loosing" or freeing others from every form of bondage and darkness imposed on humanity.

Our marriages aren't merely our personal concern but a witness to a society where divorce is commonplace and good marital relationships seem impossible. Those who are single must guard their singleness under God's hand, showing it not to be a second-rate existence but one that can have far-reaching purpose. Parenting is more than raising kids until they leave home; it is a discipling process in which they are fitted for the kingdom. Our friendships must become unconditional. That alone would make them rare, since many people view relationships in terms of what they can extract from them. And our careers should take shape according to how they affect the investment of our lives in God's kingdom.

Wherever we are, whatever we do, Jesus has given us the privilege of loosening the bonds of people who are slaves to things—either "respectable" or scandalous—that keep them from seeing Him. "The position you occupy in society is not an accidental one. You are placed where you are that you may be a preserving salt to those around, a sweet savor of Christ to all who know you."[2]

The second privilege, one of "binding," is a difficult one to embrace. It's important to understand what it is not. It's not the capricious ruling of individuals or groups outside of God's kingdom. Some, indeed many, will be ruled out of the kingdom eternally. An old preacher once said, "Never refer lightly to hell. People are really going there." Some of us talk about the judgment of others as if they deserved it, while forgetting that we do, too (Ephesians 2:1-3).

Binding refers to the difficult, sometimes painful, things that sometimes must be done to ensure the ongoing health and vitality of all phases of the kingdom of God. These things may appear to be unChristian to undiscerning eyes. Certainly they demand the kind of courage available only through the Holy Spirit.

The early church was blessed in such abundance that people had difficulty believing it. Lives were being changed dramatically, and the infant church was bonding into a fellowship deep and strong. A guy named Barnabas brought all the proceeds from a land transaction and gave it to the apostles. And then another windfall! A couple, Ananias and Sapphira, also brought money from a sale of land. But no one could have anticipated the response. After two brief confrontations with Peter, the dead bodies of both husband and wife were carried away and great fear fell on the church (Acts 5:1-11).

Most of us might consider the sin of Ananias and Sapphira to be rather petty or insignificant. They may have wanted the good opinion of the church, instead of the good opinion of God, and were willing to resort to deception to get it. Or God may have wanted them to do the same as Barnabas, and as they were unwilling to obey, they thought they could deceive both men and God by only bringing half. In any case, what they did was a far cry from rape or murder.

What the church needed was to learn a lesson about sin: All sin is deadly. Much more can be said about this incident, but suffice it to say that what appeared to be a low-grade infection was in fact a lethal disease that couldn't be allowed to go on. We can point to other seemingly harsh punishments for sin that occurred as well (Acts 8:18-24). Furthermore, the teaching of Paul's letters is sometimes hard to choke down: "I have decided to deliver such a one to Satan for the destruction of his flesh, that his spirit may be saved in the day of the Lord Jesus" (1 Corinthians 5:5); "Those who continue in sin, rebuke in the presence of all, so that the rest also may be fearful of sinning" (1 Timothy 5:20).

These examples sound especially tough in the climate of contemporary churches, where rarely do we risk hurting anyone's feelings. And so some churches spend a lot of time in cordial banalities that mask widespread evasion of serious issues and unresolved pain that go back years. People with serious spiritual pathology go on wounding others, sometimes inadvertently and sometimes not. When pressed as to why no one says anything, we claim that we do not shoot our wounded. But is it genuinely possible to heal without pain?

A member in my church was once rushed to the hospital and diagnosed as having a collapsed lung. As he told me later, "I thought I was in bad pain as I struggled for breath. But when the doctor cut an incision and forced a tube into my lung to inflate it, I thought it was all over." The doctor knew the cure would hurt more than the problem, but that is no excuse for withholding the cure. We must not shrink from the privilege of binding. The spiritual cure of individuals, churches, and other segments of the kingdom are too important.

Infections, no matter how innocuous they seem, can fester. I know one church whose credibility was utterly destroyed in the community. At crucial times either no one spoke up or everyone was too deeply embroiled in the poison to notice. I do know that the gospel of Jesus Christ was trodden underfoot in front of the dying people of that community.

Young churches especially need to carefully exercise this privilege of binding. A church planter once told me how one caustic individual had been driving people away from a home Bible study. I asked if he'd talked to this person. He replied, "No. If I do, he might leave, and we need all the bodies we can get." Christ's church never needs bodies for bodies' sake. When we close a Sunday service with the likes of Ananias, Sapphira, Alexander (2 Timothy 4:14), and Diotrephes (3 John 9), we need to reevaluate how well we have been "binding." The kingdom of God aches for courageous people who are willing to treat the wounds within the church.

WOUNDED BY THE MASTER'S LOVE

A distinct privilege not many want is that of being rebuked by Jesus. Anyone would want to enjoy the full impact of Christ's love, but His love has a prickly side: "Those whom I love, I reprove and discipline; be zealous therefore, and repent" (Revelation 3:19).

The study of the rebukes of Jesus is interesting. Sometimes they were soft (Luke 10:17-20, John 14:9); other times they struck like lightning (Matthew 16:21-23, Luke 9:54-55). But they all had distinctive marks it would be good for us to recognize.

First is to know that this is much more than a morbid preoccupation of a conscience gone awry. A righteous rebuke is the unveiling of the glory of Jesus Christ to the heart through the Holy Spirit. At times no human instrumentality is needed. At other times the individual may be utterly unaware of being the Lord's tool, or he may knowingly and courageously be doing some "binding." But whether through people or through the Spirit speaking to the heart, it is Jesus, the Lord, who speaks.

A second characteristic is a deep pain. Rebukes hurt—always. The pain will be specific and sharp; there will be no doubt over the issue. Christ the Lord doesn't mumble or avoid the truth.

Such pain from a righteous rebuke should have three distinct results. First, to someone else the matter in question may seem trivial, but the one rebuked will deeply grieve over it. Second, our pride will feel the sting when we feel a rebuke. How hard it is to comply with the Bible's warning to have a sensible or sane estimate of our capabilities. We so easily assume we must be so much farther along than we are. Then the voice of Jesus slices through our pride like a hot knife through butter. And third, we'll not soon be so quick to glibly trust ourselves. We'll be brought back to a deeper dependence on God.

A third characteristic is that Jesus' rebukes aren't meant to be wounds unto death. That's a good thing to know because they often feel like it. The cynical journalist Ambrose Bierce once wrote, "A friend is someone who stabs you in the front." To an extent, that's true. But when Jesus wounds, He wounds cleanly and only to heal. As He already said, He does it because He loves us. While we'd probably rather pass on this privilege of the kingdom of God, we need to face Jesus' tough love. Scripture warns that if anyone fails to hear the voice of Jesus in this way, he is not in God's family or His kingdom at all (Hebrews 12:5-11).

THE PRIVILEGE OF THE LOW PLACE

A man was packing his things at the close of a week-long conference. The woman who'd cleaned his room all week had just come in and was starting on the bathroom. As he went to tip her for the excellent work done, she surprised him as she stood up from scrubbing the toilet and said, "Oh, I could never take your money. You see I *get* to do this. It's my ministry!" Another privilege of God's kingdom is serving. Our reaction to this little story says a lot about how well we recognize this as a privilege.

This lady, and real serving, are enigmas to us for a couple of reasons. First, we have attached a finely differentiated value system to tasks. Much of our self-esteem is tied to what we do. If what we do doesn't seem significant in our own eyes then neither do we. It bothers us to see someone else doing something we think to be beneath him. We think he can do better than that. Maybe he can, but in serving, that's beside the point.

The second reason we fail to understand the woman gladly scrubbing toilet bowls for the glory of God is that we're often selfish. God would never call me to do anything other than what I would normally want to do anyway, would He? This alone has made large tracts of Western Christianity an ugly, nearsighted thing.

By way of contrast, our call from God is one of serving: "For even the Son of Man did not come to be served, but to serve, and to give His life a ransom for many" (Mark 10:45); "And I will most gladly spend and be expended for your souls. If I love you the more, am I to be loved the less?" (2 Corinthians 12:15).

Biblical serving doesn't esteem the task; it doesn't look for things to be glamorous, exciting, or meaningful, and therefore worthy of our effort. Serving in the kingdom of God ennobles any task, making it a privilege to take on the lowliest chore in Christ's name. The woman scrubbing toilet bowls pegged it well: We *get* to do this. There's an effortlessness to it. It's not compulsive, begrudged, or forced. It doesn't clamor for the spotlight or for applause. Rather, it is fueled by love for Christ and love for those He loves.

When you think of "great" Christians, of what do you think? Too often we look at the highly visible things. But Jesus said that the great ones in the kingdom of God are servants: "And calling them to Himself, Jesus said to them, 'You know that those who are recognized as rulers of the Gentiles lord it over them; and their great men exercise authority over them. But it is not so among you, but whoever wishes to become great among you shall be your servant; and whoever wishes to be first among you shall be slave of all'" (Mark 10:42-44).

Spiritual authority, depth, and greatness are self-authenticating. When we have to be told that these elements are present, they're usually not. When someone has to tell us how spiritual he is or what a great leader he is, he's usually not. But when these things are real, they're intuitively recognized as something remarkable.

Once when I was attending a student conference, our base for the conference was a circus tent erected on a campground. In the middle of the week a cloudburst struck the area and completely washed out the campground. Everyone's gear was either soaked or buried in mud. A guy wearing baggy bermuda shorts, a sport shirt three sizes too big, and black knee socks was slogging through the muck talking to people and helping them salvage their stuff. It was Billy Graham. The great ones in the kingdom of God may have highly visible ministries *or* they may be utterly unknown. But they are servants *par excellence*.

The woman scrubbing toilets understood something else when she said, "I *get* to do this." It wasn't just that they didn't pay her, but that they *couldn't* pay her enough to equal what she was getting out of her work. Serving in the kingdom of God is its own reward. Jesus said as much in Matthew 10:39: "He who has found his life shall lose it, and he who has lost his life for My sake shall find it." This saying is echoed five more times in the gospels (Matthew 16:25; Mark 8:35; Luke 9:24, 17:33; John 12:25).

I've always been amused to watch golfers yell, scream, and throw clubs while doing something they claim helps them relax. I too know what it is to hack and scratch my way through nine holes of missed putts and shanked drives, while making the intimate acquaintance of every sand trap on the course. But in the middle of every nine holes of frustration are one or two shots that are worthy of the pros, ones that will live in our memory for a long time. For only a few seconds everything is in alignment and even the greatest couldn't have done it better.

Every endeavor or field of performance knows this feeling of transcendence. The Christian never captures it more fully than when he or she serves. Most would say to do something unselfishly feels good. To more accurately define it, serving feels right. It feels right to spend your life on that for which it was meant to be spent.

> Their hearts sing with a strange wild joy, automatically and with no exception. We are structured for the outgoingness of the love of the Kingdom. It is our native land.[3]

For those sometimes all too brief moments, we're in sync with the performance of not Olympic athletes or renowned operatic figures but with Jesus Christ Himself. These are some of the great moments of a Christian's life—moments where God's glory is so intense that it almost has texture and taste. But to back off from serving unless we're guaranteed a reward that can be banked, polished in a trophy case, or listed on a résumé is to severely misunderstand what it means to follow Jesus.

> What God says . . . is "The life you save is the life you lose." . . . The life you clutch, hoard, guard, and play safe with is in the end a life worth little to anybody, including yourself, and only a life given away for love's sake is a life worth living. To bring his point home, God shows us a man who gave his life away to the extent of dying a national disgrace without a penny in the bank or a friend to his name. . . . He was a Perfect Fool, and anybody who thinks he can follow him without making something like the same kind of a fool of himself is laboring under not a cross but a delusion.[4]

To treasure the privilege of serving in God's kingdom is to be rich. To esteem it lightly because we're giving the cream of our lives to selfish, albeit good, things marks us as poor in the kingdom of God.

6
Making an Impact

The captain couldn't believe his eyes. Those little boats were coming right at him. Surely they'd veer away. But they didn't, and a fleet of sizable whaling ships had to zigzag chaotically through the icy water off the Aleutian Islands.

These little vessels skipping around like water bugs weren't a bunch of weekend sailors who'd accidentally wandered into the shipping lanes. Grim faces stood by the throttle of every skiff and raft. These near-collisions were no accident, but a dramatic attempt by a group named Greenpeace to stop the wholesale slaughter of whales. Placing themselves squarely between the whaling fleet and the herds of whales beyond, their message was clear: "You'll go through us before we'll let you have them."

Such defiance coming from a handful of people bobbing like corks under the hovering prows of seagoing whalers seemed ridiculous. But you couldn't help pulling for them. Part of me wanted to see the destructive technological undoing of our environment stopped, or at least hindered awhile. Another part of me loves the underdog.

But there was something more, something deeper.

People who make deep commitments to things outside of themselves radiate life. Watching them stirred me to think, *Wouldn't it be great to have that kind of dedication and courage over something?*

The early Christians were an unstoppable bunch. They explode from the second chapter of Acts like a rodeo bull from a chute, and still have full steam at the end of the book. They saw Christianity as something to be lived at full throttle—not merely a support system to strengthen or to embellish their concerns.

A deep undertow ripples through the pews of many churches. An intuitive frustration rises like an itch that's hard to scratch as people look first at their Bibles and then at themselves and ask, "Why aren't we like that?" They sense that something has gone wrong when the RV and camper show at the county fairgrounds has more life and vitality than the congregational life of the local church. The commitment, the passion, the zeal of those early Christians transcends time. It spices the pages of church history as the Spirit of God impregnates first one culture or century, then another. We could stand an epidemic of it today.

Those early Christians did not work up ill-defined enthusiasm for Jesus out of their physical nature. Their zeal for God's kingdom has recognizable elements that can and should be cultivated. But first we need a broad overview.

Following Jesus means living a life of focused intensity. Seeking first His kingdom and pressing His redemption into every crevice and cavity of creation is our ultimate reason for living (Matthew 6:33). We're not to be neutral about it. This is not armchair stuff. It moves everyone it touches. It challenges us to pit ourselves against anything and everything that opposes the kingdom of God. So be warned! Anyone who thinks he can follow Jesus Christ and know nothing of this zeal has greatly miscalculated.

ROOTS OF KINGDOM ZEAL

The primary taproot of zeal for God's kingdom is *loving Christ*. Believing the gospel message is never purely an intellectual venture. The gospel seizes our whole being with the stupendous truth that God took on human frame in order to take upon Himself the judgment our sin deserves. How can we not love Him eagerly in return?

The Apostle Paul isn't a difficult man to understand; he was in love with Christ. If, in the process, he threw away a blossoming career and became an outcast in the eyes of his former friends and associates, he didn't seem to care. Pleasing the One he loved seemed more important at the time.

I remember phoning my dad to tell him of my engagement to Gay. He said he was happy for us, but he asked us to promise to finish school first. I said, "Dad, we've got that all figured out. Remember all the money we banked for school this year? I drew it all out to buy the engagement ring and wedding bands. I'll get a *job* to raise the money for second semester." Telling him that on the phone from over four hundred miles away may be one of the smartest things I've ever done.

Paul would understand. For Paul, loving Christ was the antiphonal response to Christ's love for him. It was no mere philosophical pursuit. Being loved by Christ and loving Him in return had real spice in it. "For the love of Christ controls us, having concluded this, that one died for all, therefore all died; and He died for all, that they who live should no longer live for themselves, but for Him who died and rose again on their behalf" (2 Corinthians 5:14-15).

Christ's love gripped Paul, hemming him in on every side. He lived joyously in the grasp of that love. When the dust settled at the end of his life, something eternal remained. Writing of Paul, one man said, "The splash he

made when he fell for Christ is audible still. . . . He went his
way and wrote his marvelous . . . Christ-drunk letters. Jesus
lit the fire and Paul used it to forge for him a church."[1]

What does Christ want to forge with your life? Remember that forging can't be done at room temperature. It
requires heat. Stop worrying about how it will look, what
others might think, or what it may cost. People in love are
characteristically blind to such things.

A second root of zeal for the kingdom of God is *loving
others*. Most of us raise our antennae when we're told that
something is free, no strings attached. We know better.
Everything is conditional. There's always a price. Everyone
is just looking out for number one.

But people who love Jesus Christ don't live like that.
Reflecting over fifteen years of marriage, it's surprising to
me how Gay has shaped my life. I now care about and
appreciate things I never even noticed before. Why?
Because she cares about them. In the same way, when you
love Jesus you also begin to love what He loves. And Jesus
Christ loves people.

A friend of ours became a Christian. She was married
to a doctor and had spent a lot of time at luncheons with
friends. But Jesus changed her priorities. She soon began
cultivating friendships with the transient people who lived
in the old downtown hotels. She talked with them, brought
them food, took them shopping, and visited them in the
hospital. Everyone warned her about how dangerous it was,
but she was too busy having the time of her life to listen.

Who wants to be loved? Everyone. But some people
have never known love. They need time to recognize it for
what it is. Others have risked loving and have the scars to
prove it. They need time to rebuild trust. When we try to love
someone in difficult situations, we find that our own love, if
left to itself, is a fragile bloom that wilts when there's no

immediate response in kind.

Loving Jesus gives our love for others staying power for the long haul. The reward is worth the wait. Loving people with Christ's love gives them a small breath of air from another realm.

William Wilberforce, a political leader of England's nineteenth century, was a vibrant Christian. One summer he visited his family at their summer home. His mother dreaded the visit, having learned of his becoming a Christian (a dirty word among the aristocracy of those days). But when she saw a remarkable lightness and sweetness that replaced a vile temper, she wrote to a friend, "If this is madness, I hope he will bite us all."[2]

Jesus had this kind of positive effect on Zacchaeus, the woman at the well, and so many others. And we can, too. When it happens, don't be surprised to find even those who oppose and disagree with you pressing their noses against the window to see what's going on.

> There is a person who has profoundly disturbed my peace of mind for a long time. She doesn't know me but she continually goes around minding my business. . . . She drives me crazy. I get upset every time I hear her name or read her name or read her words or see her face. I don't even want to talk about her. . . .
>
> No shah or president or king or general or scientist or pope; no banker or merchant or cartel or oil company or ayatollah holds the key to as much power as she has. None is as rich. For hers is the invincible weapon against the evils of this earth: the caring heart . . . the eloquence of her life speaks to me. . . . I do not believe in her version of God. But the power of her faith shames me. . . . I believe in Mother Teresa.[3]

A third root of zeal for the kingdom of God is *truth*. Truth has been seriously devalued in our contemporary world. The word itself has little meaning. Maybe this is due to the feeble counterfeits peddled among us. Most types of "truth" are nothing more than seedbeds of doubt or skepticism.

Real truth is powerful stuff. It detonates people into life and action. Finding truth has an "aha!" quality about it. The second we lay our hands on it, we instinctively know we've got our hands on the terminals of something foundational in the universe.

> Jesus and his kingdom have gotten into my blood . . . and have raised my temperature, my emotions, my thinking, my outlook, my confidence, my allegiance, my everything.
>
> A very modern young man hearing me in a sophisticated drawing room meeting turned to his host and said, "That old cat knows where it is at." No credit to me. I had been sniffing around the world for half a century, sniffing for reality, and when I got a whiff of this I pounced on it.[4]

Jesus Himself *is* truth—the real thing in all its radiant power (John 14:6). Those who found Him became, not a bunch of philosophical drudges, but the most contagiously unfettered people in history. Jesus said it in John 8:32: "You shall know the truth, and the truth shall make you free." Truth yearns to be shared; it burns to be told.

But the truth that fuels zeal for God's kingdom is more finely differentiated than just truth about Jesus. It includes truth about other things as well, things like sin. Sin is no illusion or myth; it is quite real. The measure of its serious-ness is neither culture nor our personal standard of right-

eousness. The standard is the holiness of God. Sin is not
what we do; it is what we are.

> Sin cannot be limited to isolated instances or patterns
> of wrongdoing; it is something much more akin to the
> psychological term complex: an organic network of
> compulsive attitudes, beliefs and behaviour deeply
> rooted in our alienation from God.[5]

If it is not dealt with on Christ's terms, sin will kill even
the best people we know. Death, judgment, and hell await.
Words of their certainty fall from the lips of Jesus Himself.
And the ones who are dying have no idea. How can one
who knows a cure for a fatal disease keep it to himself? How
can a doctor watch someone die and make no effort to tell
the dying person what is wrong?

Loving Christ, loving others, and knowing the truth
about redemption and sin combine to create a burden of
awful weight. But we don't carry it alone. Its massive bulk
already weighs on the heart of God. Calvin Miller poetically
describes this weight:

> "And here," said Earthmaker, "is the crown of all my
> endless skies—the green, brown sphere of all my
> hopes." He reached and took the round new planet
> down, and held it to his ear.
>
> "They're crying, Troubadour," he said, "They cry
> so hopelessly. . . . Year after weary year they all keep
> crying. They seem born to weep then die. . . . It is a
> peaceless globe. Some are sincere in desperate desire
> to see her freed of her absurdity. But war is here. Men
> die in conflict, bathed in blood and greed." Then with
> his nail he scraped the atmosphere and both of them
> beheld the planet bleed.[6]

Jesus knew the truth about sin. He wept over it and pressed on to the Cross, where He beat it to death. His passion resurfaces in people like Jude, who spoke of the importance of saving others, "snatching them out of the fire" (Jude 23).

People fierce for the kingdom of God also understand the truth about justice. Sin can be corporate as well as individual. When sinful people populate structures, those structures can become sinful and victimize those they were designed to help and protect.

Social activists make us uncomfortable. Maybe we evangelicals have been preoccupied with doctrinal battles or with our own pursuit of the American dream for too long. But activism is a great part of our heritage.

A noble chapter of evangelical history was written by a group of British Christians known as the Clapham Sect. They were men in places of power who saw the grim evils of slavery and became driven to eradicate it. Living in community and fervent in evangelism, they focused their energies to this end. Some broke their health. Others lost whole fortunes or died before the day was seen. But their work and sacrifice peacefully eradicated slavery and other ills spawned by the sprawling octopus that was the Industrial Revolution.

Once again, Christians are picketing, organizing politically, demonstrating, and being arrested. Should we be doing this? It all depends. Is evangelizing the lost enough? Does God care about governments oppressing the freedom of people, millions of people without food and basic medical care? Does He care about national economies where the rich get richer and the poor get poorer? What about financial exploitation of our environment, racial prejudice, pornography, the sexual exploitation of our children, unemployment, and a hundred other things that threaten to unravel humanity? Is evangelism enough? Read and decide:

Imagine that all the population of the world were condensed to the size of one village of 100 people. In this village, 67 of the 100 would be poor; the other 33 would be in varying degrees well off. Of the total population, only seven would be North Americans. The other 93 people would watch the seven North Americans spend one-half of all the money, eat one-seventh of all the food, and use one-half of all the bath-tubs. These seven people would have ten times more doctors than the other 93. Meanwhile the seven would continue to get more and more and the 93 less. . . .

The trouble is that the wealthy seven continually try to evangelize the other 93. We tell them about Jesus and they watch us throw away more food than they can ever hope to eat. We are busy building beautiful church buildings, and they scrounge to find shelter for their families. We have money in the bank and they do not have enough to buy food for their children. All the while we tell them that our Master was the Servant of men, the Saviour who gave his all for us and bids us give all for him. . . . We are the rich minority in the world. We may be able to forget about that or consider it unimportant. The question is, can the 93 forget?[7]

We've looked at the roots necessary for zeal in the kingdom of God. When roots take hold they produce growth that can be seen. So it is with true passion for God's kingdom; it has observable signs that unmistakably mark it.

GOD-CENTERED BOLDNESS

Boldness is a clearcut mark of kingdom zeal. People who seek first the kingdom of God are bold people. This is certainly not a form of obnoxiousness or brashness. Some take a carnal delight in rebellion, in tweaking authority of any kind on the nose. Boldness for the kingdom is far more than that.

A mother and her small child went to the zoo. Preoccupied for a minute or two, the mother didn't notice the child wander off and somehow enter the wild cat habitat. Seeing her daughter inside and being eyed by a tiger, the mother dashed after the girl and arrived at about the same time as the big cat. Instinctively the mother grasped the tiger around the neck and wrestled it away from the little girl. Surprised by the uncommon ferocity of the mother, the tiger decided there were easier lunches to be had, and it retreated.

Boldness for the kingdom of God is something like that. Average people who are galvanized by a strange courage completely beyond themselves tend to tackle things that would naturally dwarf and intimidate them. They stand ready for the destruction of whatever fortresses, speculations, and lofty matters that raise their Hydra heads against God (see 2 Corinthians 10:4-5).

Let's look at a prime example of righteous boldness. Peter and John had spent quite a day at the Temple. First they'd healed a lame man, and now Peter was preaching powerfully. While he spoke, Peter heard a commotion over his shoulder. Suddenly the authorities, priests, and guards fell on them like thunder, dragged the two of them away, and locked them up.

The next day they hauled Peter and John before Annas, Caiaphas, and other high rulers for a hearing. Courts and judges can be quite intimidating. But these were the very men who indicted Jesus and engineered His murder. Why would they hesitate to snuff out a couple of fishermen who were causing problems?

Peter and John had every reason to fear for their lives. But they were too busy being on the attack. Peter stood there and boldly accused these men to their face of murdering the Messiah and proclaimed that God had overturned their blasphemous treachery, establishing Jesus Christ as the foundation of the redemption of all mankind. Furthermore, Peter said that he would preach this message wherever he could and that nothing they did would stop him.

Talk like that can get you killed. But Peter and John were released, while a room full of highly-educated religious power brokers were stunned and rocked back on their heels (Acts 4:1-23)! People with such boldness find themselves doing things they never dreamed possible. Their lives are the cauldron where the impossible is accomplished. The Holy Spirit propels them with laser-like focus to pierce anything opposing God's kingdom.

Consider boldness in a totally different setting. Four boys and I sat primed on a toboggan. They seemed nervous and were glad I was riding along. But little did they know! They had good reason to be nervous, since I'd never ridden on a toboggan before. Off we went.

In seconds we were shooting down the hill. Snow sprayed in our eyes, blinding us; I could sense we were really moving. The guys could feel it, too. Suddenly a huge oak tree that looked twenty feet thick ran out in front of us! The guys started to bail out—all except Mike. Everybody rolled off, leaving Mike on the front and me on the back.

The oak loomed over us as we whistled down the hill. Thoughts of severe injury flashed through my mind. But apparently not in Mike's. Squinting through the blowing snow, I saw him up on his knees, his face into the wind, alive with excitement as doom seemed imminent. We somehow swerved and missed the tree by inches. Mike glanced at it as we zoomed by, and yelled at me over his shoulder, "What an adventure!"

People with both feet firmly planted in the kingdom of this world are like me. As we hurtled toward the tree, I thought about the hospitalization being paid up, hoped there wouldn't be much pain when we hit, and dreaded the inconvenience of being laid up in a body cast. Security and comfort mean a lot—sometimes too much for our own good. People who are bold for the kingdom of God are like Peter and John—and Mike. They're magnificently blind to potential personal consequences. They're not reckless, but they're also not afraid.

Just as tiny coral solidify into something strong enough to rip the bottom out of most ships, these bold ones of the kingdom etch the fingerprints of God into broken lives, neighborhoods, communities, nations, cultures, and all of humanity. They're not complacent, comfortable church-going folk; they're insistent, daring, and sometimes contro-versial. But their fervor is infectious, and it tends to multiply. Suppress just one and five will spring up from the dust to take his place.

People bold for the kingdom of God are also bold in opposition to sin. Something terrible has happened to the church in many quarters. It's become a nice place. Nice people dressed in nice clothes come to a comfortable build-ing to hear a nice sermon and have friendly conversations with other nice people like themselves. So where can we go to get help slaying the monsters and sin in our lives? This toothless, impotent niceness gums away the church's rea-son for existing. The curing of souls gets delegated to the bartender at the corner tavern or to a radio talk-show host. It's unthinkable to let down the mask and tell somebody at church.

But one Sunday a young man dropped a small bomb that effectively reduced any of our rehearsed niceness to junk. I knew Rick and Cindy. They were Christians and had just become engaged. I could see the stars in their eyes.

Part of our worship service allows for prayer needs to be openly shared from the pews. That Sunday Rick raised his hand, stood, and in front of about fifty strangers said, "I want you to pray for me. I'm going to be married in a week. But I'm twenty-two years old and I'm still afraid of the dark."

Not many of us have the sheer nerve to say something like that. We've lost much of the therapeutic value of biblical confession. We've adulterated ourselves with a twisted hybrid from the psychological greenhouses of sensitivity training. We've created spiritual merit badges that make it a virtue to spill our guts. And if we can't do this, something is surely wrong with us.

In the prayer groups of even the most conservative churches, peer pressure to indulge in this kind of thing is strong. A student who had endured this brutality at his seminary told me that on command he could now rip open his soul and lay bare every inch of his being in three minutes. But when confession becomes compulsive, it brutalizes instead of healing. Another thing we've done is to give self-centered, self-pitying people a golden opportunity to more deeply ingrain and reinforce the garbage of their lives by rehearsing it under the guise of confession or sharing a prayer need.

Rick was doing neither of these things. He'd simply read James 5:16, where it says, "Therefore, confess your sins to one another, and pray for one another, so that you may be healed. The effective prayer of a righteous man can accomplish much." Some things we just can't improve on. Christianity knows nothing of bootstrap theology. As we could not save ourselves, neither can we live the Christian life without complete dependence on Christ and on other Christians. Since Rick knew he was a sinner surrounded by other sinners, admitting he had a need was no big deal.

Friends who will pray, hold us accountable to our intentions, and join us in our trials are like spiritual splints that buttress a broken soul until it can heal. We can choose to be silent because of what others might say or because we have an image to uphold. But what is disintegrating inside while we're doing that on the outside? We don't have to find fifty or sixty strangers to engage in biblical confession. Rick took a big plunge, and in doing so he honored us with incredible trust. James only said the need was for one righteous person, one listening ear.

A friend of ours once went through incredibly tough times, and we prayed regularly over the situation in detail. Recently he wrote, saying that in our last letter we had alluded to some of our own needs in a rather general way. Now he asked us to be more specific. In effect, he was saying, "Look, you turkeys, you really hung in there with us. Now open up to us so we can bless you in return."

A kick in the pants from a righteous man is often as effective and as necessary as his prayers. I immediately wrote a long letter and felt that inner release that signifies the rightness of obedience to God. A couple of things have resulted. Fresh grace immediately began lubricating our lives, bringing both light and rest. Obedience often does that. Second, we knew that this grace would not only continue but we could expect it to increase since someone cared enough to carry our hurts to the throne of God.

Rick refused to be without this kind of help. He was bold to ask for it, one sinner to another. How about us? All we have to lose is a reputation that is propped up by pride. If we risk letting it drop, we can gain a life-changing taste of something of God's kingdom. Ask God even now for that righteous man or woman, that one listening ear.

Those who are bold for the kingdom of God are also

bold in *faith*. They can believe God for what only He can do. These are determined, strong-willed people. Their spiritual kin are in the Bible, and Christ's church needs more of them.

> "The kingdom of heaven is like a treasure hidden in the field, which a man found and hid; and from joy over it he goes and sells all that he has, and buys that field. Again, the kingdom of heaven is like a merchant seeking fine pearls, and upon finding one pearl of great value, he went and sold all that he had, and bought it." (Matthew 13:44-46)

I've done time on my share of committees, some of them especially geared for long-range planning. I like doing it. It suits me. I like working methodically toward goals and planning with objectives. But somewhere in the middle of all the grids, graphs, charts, statistics, and projections, faith can be lost. All these dimensions of planning should incarnate faith. But they may not.

A college friend of mine who studied mathematics used to say, "If you can't graph it, what good is it?" It's not hard to think that way. Our church efforts have too much of the smell of man about them. Too much of what we do is entirely explainable in human terms. Even attempts at church growth can be mechanically controlled, turning small ingrown churches into large ingrown churches that would have had the exact same results had God done nothing at all.

Another reason I like working on long-range planning committees is that I don't like surprises. I not only like to know what's going to happen; I like to control it. One of the great ironies of church history is that the great movements of the Spirit of God almost always found the fiercest opposition from clergy and other religious leaders. Down beneath much of their arguing lies a fear of not being in control.

People bold in faith for God's kingdom are always believing God for the most unheard of, outrageous things. My desire to tone these people down is sometimes condescending and selfish. They embarrass me. While my instincts rush to say that faith is no excuse for presumption, their spirit rebukes me that neither should planning and organization be a cloak for unbelief. God always wants to do bigger things than I can envision—things that include but don't require me. One man said, "There is an enormous gap between what we think we can do and what God calls us to do. Our ideas of what we can do or want to do are trivial; God's ideas for us are grand."[8]

People with a bold faith instinctively grasp this concept. In preparing for our long-range planning work, we spent a weekend with a church that is doing marvelous work. Their staff talked with us about church structure and philosophy of ministry. We filled our notebooks with good things that could be graphed, charted, and projected.

We discovered their real secret when we worshiped with them. At the end of most other churches' services, people do some disturbing things. They shuffle around, gather coats and other belongings, talk among themselves, and do a hundred other things that indicate that everything is over and that it's almost time to leave. All of this activity seems innocuous, but it completely quenches the Holy Spirit. It may be the outward expression of a heart that doesn't expect God to do much. And that perspective is seldom disappointed.

But this was not the case with these people. As the service came to a close, the atmosphere was charged with a sense of expectation. No one rummaged for coats or purses. Our committee was scattered throughout the room and, comparing notes later, we noticed that everyone was doing one of two things. Many prayed. But many others stood on tiptoe to see who would be making some kind of decision for Christ. They fully expected God's Spirit to do something remarkable. There hadn't been a Sunday in the five years leading up to our visit that they'd been disappointed.

I will continue to do long-range planning, but I hope to never do it without people like these, or the ones described in the book of Acts. It's convicting, even threatening, but worth it.

> These men did not make "acts of faith," they believed; they did not "say their prayers," they really prayed. They did not hold conferences on psychosomatic medicine, they simply healed the sick. . . . No one can read this book without being convinced that there is Someone here at work besides mere human beings. Perhaps because of their very simplicity, perhaps because of their readiness to believe, to obey, to give, to suffer, and if need be to die, the Spirit of God found what he must always be seeking—a fellowship of men and women so united in love and faith, that he can work in them and through them with the minimum of let or hindrance.[9]

FEAR OF BEING UNFIT

Both the American craze for physical fitness and its love affair with the automobile unfold almost at my doorstep every day. On a nearby street, seasoned joggers glide effortlessly along, while novices in brightly colored warm-ups stagger down the street gasping for air. All the while new sports cars, customized vans, and even rolling conglomerates of body putty and rust zoom by.

We spend billions on our bodies—slimming them down, perfuming and deodorizing them, dressing them sharply. And don't we pamper our cars? They are far more than a means of transportation. Luxurious accessory packages, customized paint, and powerful engines tell of personal identities entwined with machines.

How characteristic of us to give such diligent care to things that will not last. What care are we giving to our souls? If we fed ourselves physically as often as we did spiritually, what kind of shape would we be in? While we cannot always recognize people who are passionate for God's kingdom by the car they drive or by how well they jog, they strive to maintain solid tone in their spiritual life. And they do this for three reasons.

First, they want nothing to erode their personal relationship with Christ. Knowing Christ is the crown jewel of the kingdom of God. Seasoned Christians know this intuitively. Wanting God merely for what He can give is a gross spiritual miscarriage. Why keep on battling temptation and sin? Why press on in service that shows neither results nor hope? Why keep banging our heads on obedience? Just the honor of knowing Christ inexorably draws us back. We wouldn't lose Him for anything.

Second, lovers of God's kingdom never want anything in their lives to smear Christ or His church. If we want to avoid sin only because of its sometimes painful consequences, we're in for a rough ride. Our own fear of getting caught isn't strong enough motivation for the long haul. When we genuinely love someone, that process of loving changes us. Genuinely loving Christ and the church, His bride, spontaneously breeds a desire to live in a way that never cheapens or misrepresents Him in any way. Those who are on fire for the kingdom of God are living signposts to the truth.

Sir Herbert Edwardes served magnificently as a soldier and administrator in India in the mid-nineteenth century. As a Christian, he believed it was his ministry to bring peace and justice to a land being ripped to pieces in bloody tribal and religious wars. After a lifetime of service and success, he died in 1869 while on sick leave in Scotland.

When the news of Sir Herbert's death reached India, an old man went to knock on the door of a missionary. He said, "I lived with Sir Herbert all the years he has been in India and I followed him everywhere. My sahib was such a good man. He can't have made a mistake in his religion. Will you teach me his religion? For I should like to believe what he believed."[10] Can anyone look at us and be moved to say these things? Or is someone perhaps going to spurn Christ because of us?

Third, kingdom people strive to live so as to always be usable in Christ's service. Paul marveled at the honor of serving God. He also feared the possibility of falling into such moral and spiritual disrepair that he would lose this honor: "I thank Christ Jesus our Lord, who has strengthened me, because He considered me faithful, putting me into service" (1 Timothy 1:12). "Therefore I run in such a way, as not without aim; I box in such a way, as not beating the air; but I buffet my body and make it my slave, lest possibly, after I have preached to others, I myself should be disqualified" (1 Corinthians 9:26-27).

Readiness for ministry is to be guarded. People we serve come to trust us. Failing that trust wounds more than just one. Our college marching band practiced on a field without yard lines. Long elastic strips were spaced five yards apart and worked fine as long as all the marchers lifted their feet. Inevitably someone would drag his feet and kick up one of the strips. Not only that person but a few on each side would fall as well. When we fall we always take those we serve with us. They become hurt. They are not immune.

Serving also spoils us for mere pew sitting. When we discover the open secret that those who lose their lives are indeed the ones who find them, we realize that we've tapped into a main source of joy, strength, and power in the Christian life. It can be heady stuff. Disqualifying ourselves through spiritual slovenliness not only discredits our Savior and wounds others; we also severely impoverish ourselves.

In older churches, the pulpit is often raised high above the floor and enclosed in a box-like structure. A mother and daughter sat in one of these churches listening to a fiery old Scot. He became more agitated as the sermon went on, waving his arms, pacing back and forth, his voice rising. The little girl became uneasy as the Spirit of God welded man and message together, and the man thunderously drove each point home from his box in the air. "Mommy," she whispered, "what happens if he gets out?"

Christianity in monotone simply isn't credible. A faith of moderation that blends into the woodwork of our culture betrays the message of Jesus Christ. A religious niceness painted in hues of gray entices no one. Beliefs that never lead to action testify to the fear and unbelief at the core of much going on right now in many churches.

But what if something changed? What if someone who loved Christ regardless of the consequences showed up in our skin? What if someone who wept over a lost and dying planet the way Jesus did started looking through our eyes?

What if someone who seethed with God's outrage over the injustice and suffering of this world started using our hands and feet? What if the Spirit of God roused us from the shameful complacency plaguing us and raised us up as lions ready to battle for God's kingdom? Throwing our stuffy dignity as well as our desires for control and comfort to the wind, what would happen if we got out of the box?

7

An Appetite for God's Will

———◆———

It was lunchtime on the loading dock. Three of us sat enjoying the sun and having a blue-collar philosophical discussion. As we talked about spiritual things, I discovered that Scott was into transcendental meditation and that Jack believed deeply in astrology. Scott said, "All I want is to be happy." A happy life, for him, was to not hurt anyone, and to have both a reasonable degree of comfort and a minimal degree of pain.

While we might change the details of his definition, who does not want to be happy? Joseph Fort Newton said, "Every man has a train of thought on which he rides when he is alone. The dignity and nobility of his life, as well as his happiness, depend upon the direction in which that train is going, the baggage it carries and the scenery through which it travels."

The indispensables someone packs in his mental baggage always include desires and appetites, the measure of what we think will bring happiness and fulfillment. Christians are no exception. But instead of fixing our hopes for happiness on the same things as everyone else, the Christian should find his appetite for the world's securities, goodies, and other incentives diminished and spoiled as he grows deeper and stronger in God's grace.

One of the wonders of becoming a Christian is to watch the spontaneous kindling of new desires and appetites. Those setting out for the kingdom of God delightfully discover that Joseph Newton's mental train not only changes direction but takes on new baggage as well. A man shook his head in amazement as he said to me, "Before I was a Christian I lived to see how much money I could make. Now I live to see how much I can give away."

Jesus Christ leaves us in no doubt as to the shape of these new appetites. He encapsulated them in the Beatitudes of the Sermon on the Mount. The focal point of happiness for the Christian is the blessing of God. The blessing of God that Jesus describes here (Matthew 5:3-12) is a far cry from the nebulous term some throw in as a postscript to praying when they say "bless the missionaries."

To bless means literally to make happy. But as we Christians try to superimpose our own private expectations or baptize our attachment to this world's goods into spiritual respectability, we always become disappointed and disillusioned. God is under no obligation to bless on our terms. The blessing of God sits like a jewel perpetually mounted in the setting of His sovereignty. God alone, as our sovereign Creator and Redeemer, knows what we need to make us truly happy and blessed.

We often disguise a want or craving as a need, and then we pout when it's not met. We witlessly try to fool a sovereign God. He wisely overrides our folly, and if our hindsight is clear, we should be glad. He blesses as He alone knows best. For those who seek first His kingdom and live not to please themselves but for His glory, that is enough. For they see the doing of the will of God as their meat and drink.

THE HAPPY POOR

Jesus said, "Blessed are the poor in spirit, for theirs is the kingdom of heaven" (Matthew 5:3). Some have taken this beatitude out of context and tried to say that the poor have a unique capacity to trust in God because they have nothing else in which to trust. But there is something totally different in view here. Poverty is neither a virtue, nor is it necessarily an aid to faith. Anyone watching a father use five dollars to buy lottery tickets that could have put socks on the bare feet of his kids to protect them against winter knows that materialistic hopes plague the poor as well as the rich.

In the Beatitudes, Christ is really giving a broad view of the citizenship requirements of the kingdom of God. The one who is truly happy and blessed and who will receive God's kingdom is the one who knows for a fact that his personal goodness, his successes and achievements, have no currency or influence with a holy and righteous God. The concern for self-esteem diminishes. Our concern is to esteem the King.

How can the poor in spirit be "blessed" or happy? Because the pockets of the human spirit are turned out empty at the foot of the cross of Christ. God has both judged and pardoned our sin there. Christ took on Himself the punishment we deserve while we receive the kind of total forgiveness, cleansing, and righteousness we do not deserve. No matter what success or achievement may come to us, if we are truly poor in spirit, then we know that we will never be more than debtors to the grace of God.

We can walk into any church, large or small, and know beyond doubt that there is not a decent person there. All churches everywhere are filled with the people whose sin murdered Christ. One mark of spiritual awakening is that when the Spirit comes in power, even the most respectable people become wounded and grieved over the seriousness of their sin. When Peter's sermon on Pentecost confronted the crowd, no one raised a hand and said, "You can't mean me. I'm a scout leader, and I serve on the school board."

One cannot simultaneously be poor in spirit and full of self. Something has gone awry when Christians squabble because what they perceive as their place, position, or honor hasn't been recognized. The energy that people who believe in Jesus spend on getting their way and holding on to power is frightening. Blessed is the man who genuinely lives in light of the knowledge that apart from the grace of God he is nothing.

When asked the secret of the Salvation Army's success, William Booth replied, "We have no reputation to lose."[1] We may not have graced the cover of *Time* or *Newsweek* or had reporters lining up at our door, but most of us have a reputation of respectability (in our own eyes at least) that we could stand to lose. Too many professing Christians live as if they're almost good enough not to need redemption.

Sometimes there are hidden motives. Our concern over title, position, and power in the church may be more than self-aggrandizement. It may be a cloak to disguise wrong.

A department store manager was suspected of stealing merchandise from his store. When confronted with the evidence, he replied with an artificially pained voice, "How can you even suspect me of such a thing? Why, I'm a deacon at the First Baptist Church." Whatever the case, we must come to know that our achievements, successes, and reputation do not impress God.

A friend of mine visited a church where everything was engraved with the names of the donors. Every square in the sidewalk, every pew, had a donor's name prominently displayed. In contrast, the poor in spirit who will someday walk the streets of the New Jerusalem (Revelation 21:10-27) do not expect to spend eternity gawking at little brass plates telling who donated the jasper walls, underwrote the gates of pearl, or funded the streets of gold. As with all God's work, man has nothing to contribute; it is all of mercy and grace. The ones who know this now while they're living in the clay of daily life are blessed.

A TIME FOR LONG FACES

Blessings sometimes come strangely wrapped. We drink deeply from the spirit of the age when we can see happiness only through pleasurable lenses. Tim Hansel said, "One of the greatest tragedies of our modern civilization is that you and I can live a trivial life and get away with it." One of the signs of such a life is defining happiness solely in terms of fun things crossing our path.

But pain is the blessing that keeps us in touch with reality. It deepens us and helps us focus by reminding us that we are neither invincible nor immortal. Building on the first beatitude, Jesus Christ rebuked the self-centered pleasure seeker in us all when He said, "Blessed are those who mourn, for they shall be comforted" (Matthew 5:4).

The mourning described here is not the grieving of the bereaved, but the grieving of the repentant. One of the defects of much contemporary Christian belief is the severing of confession of sin from repentance. Sometimes our confession seems flippant, begrudged, and without feeling. Then when we mourn, it has a selfish tinge to it. Some people mourn over sin simply because the emotional euphoria of feeling "sin-free" has been lost. We tend to regret how it affects our lives.

But we don't experience the kind of mourning Jesus describes until we grieve over what our sin does to *God*. It isn't enough to admit how poor in spirit we are if we have never seen the full cost of our poverty of spirit to God. God has made Himself vulnerable to the beings He created in His image. By choosing to love them, He's opened Himself to being hurt, being rejected.

As a parent, I understand some of the pain fathers and mothers expose themselves to just through loving their children. I've known courageous parents pushed to the brink of insanity by wayward children, yet they still loved through hailstorms of pain. Doesn't God likewise suffer at our hands through our continual rebellion? Listen to His pain over the people of Israel:

> I took them in My arms; but they did not know that I healed them. I led them with cords of a man, with bonds of love, and I became to them as one who lifts the yoke from their jaws; and I bent down and fed them. . . .
>
> How can I give you up, O Ephraim? How can I surrender you, O Israel? How can I make you like Admah? How can I treat you like Zeboiim? My heart is turned over within Me, all My compassions are kindled. (Hosea 11:3-4,8)

God carries not only the pain of facing the rebellion of man but also the pain of giving His only Son to redeem them. On the cross Jesus cried out, "My God, My God, why hast Thou forsaken Me?" (Matthew 27:46, Mark 15:34). What was it like for the Father to listen to those words fall from the lips of His Son? A poetic telling of Satan's railing in the face of God at the Cross tells it powerfully:

> I have you crying, Earthmaker. You can never glory in your universal riches, for I have made you poor. And

there is none to pity you. Everyone you made has retired to eat and drink away their absurd holiday, and when they wake up in the morning their great machine will have done its work. You lie at man's caprice and wait for him to break your heart. . . . Earthmaker is crying at the mercy of his earth.

You started crying when they broke his hands. Can it be that the agony which plunges you in grief can wash my soul with joy?

Look how he dies. Cry, Creator, Cry! This is my day to stand upon the breast of God and claim my victory over love. You lost the gamble. In but an hour your lover will be pulp upon the gallows. Did you tell him when his fingers formed the world, that he would die on Terra, groaning with his hands crushed and whimpering in my great machine?[2]

We have never truly mourned until we embrace the hideous truth that we are responsible for the Crucifixion, and then deeply grieve over it. Our sin, yours and mine, murdered the Son of God and crushed the heart of the Father. Spiritual help, even comfort, is what is promised for all who recognize their poverty of spirit and then mourn. A full pardon of God is freely given to—and deeply penetrates—a life that mourns.

Once we know the full impact of our sin upon God and its cost to Jesus Christ, subsequent sin can never be viewed casually. Keeping this knowledge in front of us is a great deterrent to sin and a spur to growth. Looking back over history, some people have been amused at the remorse reflected in diaries and biographies over seemingly insignificant events or passing thoughts. They reason that the authors must be victims of overly scrupulous consciences or possibly are introspective to a morbid degree. Actually, their sensitivity is a mark of good health.

I saw a jewelry display in a museum protected by a security system so sensitive that sometimes dust particles would trigger the alarm system. The Holy Spirit has a similar effect on the conscience. The Spirit sensitizes it to where actions and thoughts once seen as insignificant are recognized to be quite serious sin.

Anyone with a calloused conscience that has never known tears must ask himself what he really knows of the redemption of Christ. A murderer showing no remorse before the judge outrages us. What must God feel when claimants to the cross of Christ never show remorse, poverty of spirit, or mourning?

Mourning as Jesus described it has an even broader focus. It grieves over other people and situations outside the kingdom of God.

The wandering people of Israel hadn't seen Moses for days. He'd gone to the mountain to meet with God. Agitated, they pressured Aaron to consent to the making of a golden calf. A drunken spectacle resulted, something so outrageous that it caused both God and Moses to explode in anger. Justice fell swiftly. About three thousand idolatrous partyers fell to the sword.

God offered to start all over again with just Moses and make a great nation from him. Moses could have been rid of all those complaining, fickle people once and for all. But as the bodies were being carried away, Moses pleaded, "But now, if Thou wilt forgive their sin—and if not, please blot me out from Thy book which Thou has written" (Exodus 32:32). Moses absolutely bound himself to the destiny of these sinful people. If God would not forgive them, he did not want to live to see it.

Mourning over our sin breeds brokenness and power. Mourning over others' sin and over the sins of society breeds the tenacity of a bulldog. How else could we explain the dogged determination some Christians show when they see no results, or when they are called not to the spectacular but to the mundane?

Early in his ministry in India, William Carey saw no one brought to Christ for six years. Few mission boards today would continue support either to a missionary or to an area yielding so little results. But Carey knew he was doing the will of God and his heart was broken. He mourned for the people of India.

People who try to serve Christ will eventually get their feelings hurt and feel unappreciated at times. While everyone needs to be loved and appreciated by others, these should not be the drive wheels of people who mourn. Their momentum should be perpetually stoked from within by the Spirit-induced empathy for the spiritual, emotional, and physical pain of those around them. Those who mourn shouldn't need to feel constantly fulfilled, excited, or propped up by the praise of others. They resiliently press on when others may quit.

The real tenacity of those who mourn is reserved for prayer. They are intercessors without equal. Here it was that Moses bound himself to the Israelites and refused God's offer to be made a great nation if they did not survive. Nehemiah, the rebuilder of the walls of Jerusalem after captivity, stood welded in prayer to the lives of discouraged Israelites he'd never met. We see in Nehemiah 1 that he prayed with pronouns like "us," "we," and "our." Intercessors are like that. They never say, "Lord, could You help those people? They have a problem. It's not really my problem. I've never been so stupid as to get myself into a predicament like that."

A Christian leader recently noted that, although many ministries are hurting with budget shortfalls, the unavailability of funds is not the real problem. The dearth of prayer in Western Christianity—like a severed spinal cord—is to blame for the lethargy and powerlessness in many corners of the church. While we might want to deny this problem, the evidence is too much against us.

How often have we said "I'll pray for you" and forgotten to do it? Shamefully, sometimes we never even intended to do it, since "I'll pray for you" has become a convenient exit from situations of all kinds that we're uncomfortable with. At other times it's merely a verbal throwaway used to fill empty silence with something that sounds spiritual.

Even when we do pray, it can be a perfunctory duty. We can pray over the most serious things, only to completely forget about them within minutes because we've reverted to a preoccupation with our own business. We can neither praise God for the answer or persevere if it delays since the request is completely gone from our minds and hearts.

Jill will always live in my heart as a rebuke against this problem. She was part of a Bible study I led as a college student. One night when Jill came to the study, we knew immediately that she was very sick. We tried to get her to go back to her dorm and to bed, but Jill was adamant about staying. As the study closed, we prayed for her. Afterward, I opened my eyes and said, "Jill, don't even ask God again to heal you." A remark like that was very unlike me. Even as I said it I thought, *Dave, what a stupid thing to say.*

The next day I was sitting at lunch when two guys from the study walked up wearing shy grins. One said, "Have you seen Jill today?"

"No, why?" I asked.

"The Lord healed her last night," they said.

"He what?!"

I was an older Christian, more mature (supposedly), and these guys I was discipling expected me to hear the news with the calm assurance of one who had prayed in faith. But my response betrayed my tacit unbelief. Jill had been healed, and in a dramatic supernatural way. And I was shocked. But wasn't that what I asked for? Hadn't God just answered our prayers? The fact is that until those guys walked up at lunch, I hadn't given Jill a thought since we walked out of our Bible study the night before. People who mourn do not pray that way.

George Müller set up orphanages first in Bristol and then all over England to care for the many homeless children who were nothing more than flotsam of the urban poverty generated by the Industrial Revolution. Müller was a man of great faith who told no one but God of his needs.

A friend once learned that Müller had prayed almost twenty years for two friends to become Christians. "You don't really believe," he said, "that these two will come to Christ if they haven't done so by now!"

Müller bristled in reply, "Do you think God would have wasted my time praying for these men all these years if He did not intend to save them?" One came to Christ shortly before George Müller's death, the other shortly after. People who mourn not only pray but sink their teeth into the need, refusing to let go until the need is met.

Our natural inclination is to link sensitivity levels to proximity. A thousand people dying in floods during the monsoons in Bangladesh is a real tragedy. But it doesn't hit our emotions with the same impact as when the neighbor's kid lies in the hospital after sideswiping a telephone pole. People who mourn develop God's large capacity for the pain of others. It doesn't matter if it's one person or millions of people. They can be across the street or on the other side of the globe.

A.B. Simpson, the noted pastor and missions leader, was seen in his study praying. Kneeling by a corner of his desk, Simpson embraced a globe and was weeping profusely. Before we brand Simpson as being an eccentric, we should examine what the Spirit of God forged with his life and then look at what currently is rising out of our own.

Godly mourning gives birth to compassion for others, a dimension that makes for effective ministry. People who have carried pain—either their own or others'—have gone through the rite of passage into another crushed life. Some Christians have remarkable gifts, extensive biblical knowledge, and a high degree of proficiency in their spiritual disciplines. But with all of this technical success, their lives still exude a coldness like polished marble.

One day when I was visiting a man who'd had knee surgery, I noticed that his ankle was badly swollen and discolored, so I asked about it. While we were talking, the man's doctor came to check on the knee. He walked to the bed, gripped the man's swollen ankle and straightened the leg. The patient shot up out of the bed cursing. Surprised, the doctor asked if the knee still hurt, only to be told about the ankle.

What was just a slip up for this doctor is a lifestyle for some people. Their attempts to alleviate pain only increase it. Having never been genuinely wounded over their own sin, they tend to be superficial or condescending when addressing the sin of others. Having never been broken on the wheel of their own need, they are often patronizing or naive toward the needs of others.

I just learned of a man whose family is having hard times. Out of groceries, his wife wanted to go to the local food pantry for help. From sheer pride, the husband not only refused to let her go but almost refused when another couple went to get food and offered to share the surplus with them. This man is in seminary preparing for the ministry. Unless he changes and softens, his actual capacity for ministry will remain shallow.

It's good to embrace our pain of body, mind, and soul, and our needs, both material and spiritual—to own them. Such a perspective kills pride, softens the heart, and helps us develop a taste for grace. The people who are best at sharing saving and ministering grace are those who have drunk deeply of it themselves. Note Paul's words on this:

> [God] comforts us in all our affliction so that we may be able to comfort those who are in any affliction with the comfort with which we ourselves are comforted by God. For just as the sufferings of Christ are ours in abundance, so also our comfort is abundant through Christ. (2 Corinthians 1:4-5)

Jose Iturbi, the great pianist, was asked to listen to a young prodigy who was drawing raves from the critics. As the young man practiced on stage, Iturbi entered the rear of the darkened concert hall and sat down to listen. How surprised the boy was to look up from the keyboard and see the great master walking down the aisle.

After brief introductions, the young man waited anxiously to hear Iturbi's evaluation of his playing. Jose Iturbi smiled warmly and said, "Son, you have a marvelous talent. Your technique is flawless and your interpretation is innovative. There is only one thing you lack." Seeing the question mark in the boy's eyes, Iturbi said gently, "Son, you need to cry a little."

Because of our inclination to quit when God wants us to press on, because of our absorption with self that pulls us from prayer for others, and because of our own pride that makes us callous in dealing with the needs of others—we need to cry a little. As He went to the cross, Jesus said to the weeping women who followed Him, "Stop weeping for

Me, but weep for yourselves" (Luke 23:28). Because of judgment that is deserved yet undeservedly averted at a fearful price, and because untold millions suffer in countless ways outside the light of Christ's redemption, we need to weep on a regular basis. Great things of the kingdom of God open to those who freely own being poor in spirit and mourn over that poverty. If we don't start here, we can only end up deceiving ourselves with a brittle goodness, the stuff of which Pharisees are made. How much better to face the truth and take in deep drafts of grace. If we do, we'll be astonished at the people who will beat a path to the door of our life, thirsty for the same.

LAYING ASIDE THE WORLD'S POWER

We sat in Mike's living room talking about Christ. "To be honest, Dave," he said, "I think I'm looking for a god more after my own tastes." I'd often seen Mike's name and picture in the paper. He was a young entrepreneur, a mover and a shaker. He'd won every business and community award. Mike's life was a cauldron of lust for power, ambition, and self-assertiveness, and he liked it that way. I wasn't surprised that he would not want Christ, since it was Jesus Christ who said, "Blessed are the gentle, for they shall inherit the earth" (Matthew 5:5).

Gentleness, or meekness, has nothing to do with being a doormat. No one would think of Jesus Christ, Paul, or Peter as doormats. Biblical meekness describes the liberating lack of preoccupation with self. It isn't an expression of weakness, but a manifestation of power.

The prototype is Jesus Himself. When the mob came to arrest Him in Gethsemane, He went willingly after securing freedom for the disciples. He then endured without complaint a trial rigged with the slander of false witnesses. We would have demanded a lawyer and every nerve in our body would have screamed for vindication.

After Jesus suffered spitting and beating, refusing to plead with Pilate for His life, He was crucified in disgrace with the taunts of His accusers ringing in His ears as He died. They said, "He saved others; He cannot save Himself. . . . Let Him now come down from the cross, and we shall believe in Him" (Matthew 27:42). He could have. In fact, if Jesus had unloosed His power right then and there, the armament payload of a squadron of F-14s would have been useless against Him, let alone the puny swords that hung at the waists of the Roman guards.

Jesus' life is a picture of power present but under restraint, subjugated to a greater end—the will of the Father. Jesus lacked neither the courage to stand up for Himself nor the opportunity. But He refused to do so. Meekness and boldness do not contradict each other. People who seek God's kingdom are surely bold toward God and toward those who need Him. Biblical meekness describes how we ought to be toward ourselves—being freed from the gravitational field of our ego. It surfaces in many ways.

The Son of God did not consider His greatness something to be held on to at any cost (Philippians 2:5-8). So it is with those who are meek. Some people view those in full-time Christian work as individuals who can't do anything else. Most Christian workers I know are very capable of being successful in secular fields; some actually were. Even the Apostle Paul had a brilliant career stretching out in front of him when he forfeited everything for Christ. Seven brilliant students at Cambridge University left the hope of affluent careers behind for China in the 1880s. They were hailed as heroes then.

If people today make that decision to follow Christ into

a unique calling, even Christian family and friends may wonder about pursuing a career with poor prospects for a sound financial future. They may also be glad it wasn't *them* God called. The meek are liberated from the compelling need to make their mark in some career. They long to leave *God's* mark.

Meekness shows up best, however, not in our relinquished ambitions but in our relationships. While we strive to live lives that please God, there is no desire within a meek person to prove his critics or other antagonists wrong. Some critics will be telling the truth. But even when they're not, the biblically meek don't lie awake at night with their stomachs churning in anger over slander or unjust criticism they cannot silence. God sees and understands, and He will judge fairly. This frees them to honestly love and serve their opponents. When we recognize this aspect of meekness, we are better able to understand some tough Scriptures:

> If your enemy is hungry, give him food to eat; and if he is thirsty, give him water to drink; for you will heap burning coals on his head, and the LORD will reward you. (Proverbs 25:21-22)

> "Do not resist him who is evil; but whoever slaps you on your right cheek, turn to him the other also." (Matthew 5:39)

> For what credit is there if, when you sin and are harshly treated, you endure it with patience? But if when you do what is right and suffer for it you patiently endure it, this finds favor with God. For you have been called for this purpose, since Christ also suffered for you, leaving you an example for you to follow in His steps, who committed no sin, nor was

any deceit found in His mouth; and while being
reviled, He did not revile in return; while suffering,
He uttered no threats, but kept entrusting Himself to
Him who judges righteously. (1 Peter 2:20-23)

A man witnessing on the streets of San Francisco
stopped a young woman and began to strike up a conversation. As soon as the girl could see where the conversation
was going, she shouted, with hate flashing in her eyes, "You
talk about forgiveness! Well I'm a lesbian, a prostitute, and
on drugs." With that she spat on him and slapped his face.
"What does your stupid Jesus think about that?"

Most of us would be looking for a policeman. Some
might even retaliate. All of us would be angry. The young
man just looked up at her with eyes brimming with tears and
replied, "You're no worse than me, and Christ's love has
changed my life. What makes you think you've cornered the
market on sin?"

The world views the biblically meek as losers. The
entrepreneurs and power brokers can see only a bottom
line that's in the red. You never close the deal, show a profit,
or climb the ladder by living that "meek" way. That's for
losers!

So what's the payoff? The meek will rule with Jesus.
They will judge angels and adjudicate over galaxies. They
will inherit the earth. What's in it for them? For those so
forgetful of themselves because they were so intent on the
glory of God—absolutely everything!

DESIRE FOR A NEW HEART

Some people will go to great lengths to get a fresh start. We
take a new job or move hundreds of miles. Sometimes the
change is exactly what is needed. But in many other cases,

after making all the external moves we can, we begin to see the same old beasts resurfacing in our lives.

When our problems are of the heart rather than of our setting, we could move to one of the moons of Jupiter but still be the same old person. So, what's the answer? How *can* the human heart get a fresh start? Jesus not only gives us the answer, but He describes another appetite possessed by people who set their hearts on His kingdom: "Blessed are those who hunger and thirst for righteousness, for they shall be satisfied" (Matthew 5:6). The righteousness Jesus describes here should be understood in two ways.

One is from a *legal* standpoint. A man who knows himself to be spiritually poor and mourns over that poverty knows also that he is guilty. A girl went to a counselor complaining of guilt feelings she couldn't shake. It seems she was living with her boyfriend and when asked about it, she said, "I can't understand it. Living together is accepted now. Most of my friends do and our parents support us. So why do I still feel guilty?" Her wise counselor replied, "You feel guilty because you have real guilt."

Guilt is an objective state, not a subjective feeling. Biblically, we are guilty because we've violated the laws of a holy, sovereign God, who is the judge of all mankind. We are guilty regardless of what our society condones or forbids, regardless of whether we even feel guilty or not.

The legal dimension of righteousness is captured beautifully by the well-fitting theological word *imputation*. It means on one hand that all our sin is placed on Jesus Christ, marked down to His account, and that He fully pays the penalty on the cross that is rightly ours. On the other hand, the sinlessness of Christ is marked down most undeservedly on our account. God can declare us not guilty and regard us as without sin because of the atoning sacrifice of Christ. Because of this legal arrangement before

God, we are justified by faith.

The second dimension of this righteousness that believers hunger for is *personal.* According to the legal arrangement of justification, God regards believers as sinless because of the sacrifice and merit of Christ. But we cannot stop there. A righteousness in legal standing alone is not biblical righteousness. Another term, sanctification, describes the multifaceted and lifelong process in which the Holy Spirit actually produces a sinless nature that grows right up through our personality.

We are in desperate need of the kind of righteousness that can be seen and experienced. One of the main reasons that the phrase "born again" has become such a prostituted and redundant term is that the people who use it the most show so little evidence of its truth. Being a new creation in Christ is more than a matter of standing alone; it is an observable reality.

Among evangelical ranks today, I see a serious and unrealized crisis of confidence in the power of the gospel. It's not that our belief in Christ is deficient. No, He still rises as an unvanquished conqueror from our Bibles. But if His Spirit lives in our hearts, why are so many of us virtually unchanged people even after many years in Christ?

We tend to feel intimidated by some of the deeply ingrained pathologies of sin surfacing in our society. While we are glad to hear victorious testimonies of former homosexuals, Satanists, drug addicts, and others, many of us are glad deep inside that these people attended church somewhere else while they were wrestling with those monsters. After all, if we've seen no change over the years in our lives, how much confidence can we expect to have in addressing someone else's sin?

This righteousness that can be seen is a great encouragement. I will never forget the morning after I became a

Christian. I walked down the dormitory stairs passing a guy named Phil. Phil was a thief and desperado who was despised throughout the building. I hated the guy, and if I ever had to speak to him it was only to curse at him. As we passed on the landing, I looked at him and said, "Hi, Phil! How are you?" He was as shocked as I was.

Dumbfounded, we stared at each other, then moved on, each in his own state of disbelief. Christ could not have performed a greater miracle had He raised someone from the dead in front of my eyes. Where did *that* come from? It came out of me, but it certainly wasn't me.

Today there is plenty that still needs to be flushed out. The benchmarks of tangible victory like that first one keep me going. At the Cross, Satan and his demons made their most malignant and frenzied attempt to destroy God's kingdom, only to wind up with the Son of God's foot on their necks while the lifeless forms of sin and death lay crushed in each nail-pierced hand. The Spirit of such a Holy One supernaturally indwells your personality as a Christian.

Don't shrink from whatever God's Spirit may pinpoint, no matter how often you've failed. Christ only raises these vestiges of sin, as uncomfortable as they may be to us, in order to lay them dead at our feet. And so we not only walk on in awe to the next struggle, but do it eagerly as we see something of another realm, another dimension, forming in our personality.

Please notice, though, that Christ promises satisfaction to those who hunger and thirst. This pursuit of righteousness is no mere pastime. It's not something done in idle moments while we're resting from our more important pursuits. It's meat and drink. People who crave righteousness the way the body craves food and water always stand out as being different.

First of all, people who hunger and thirst for righteousness are tough on themselves. Most of us tend to be tough on others. We seldom doubt that we understand others' motives or know the course of action that should have been taken. By contrast, we tend to be indulgent with ourselves—gracious toward our own mistakes, prone to set ourselves in the best light, generous toward our worldly appetites. But those hungering and thirsting for righteousness turn this mindset upside down. They are tough on themselves. Their refusal to spare themselves nurtures a resilient and sterling honesty that sets them apart. They know that their worst enemy lives inside their own shirt.

> God, harden me against myself,
>   The coward with pathetic voice
>   Who craves for ease and rest and joy.
> Myself, arch-traitor to myself,
>   My hollowest friend,
>   My deadliest foe,
>   My clog, whatever road I go.[3]

Because they are tough on themselves, people who hunger and thirst for righteousness are *transparent*. They do not withhold any area of their lives from Christ's gaze. They stand ready to respond when Christ touches even the most cherished dreams of their lives. They understand the call to obedience that drove Abraham to offer Isaac, his son, as a sacrifice (Genesis 22:1-8). In Abraham's case, God stopped the knife. But in the life of a Christian, sometimes the knife must fall.

My grandfather wears a hearing aid. Sometimes he finds it very useful. When he's around someone he doesn't want to listen to, he just turns it off. The average person is like my grandfather. Our spirits are too often intentionally deaf lest we hear God speak about things we cherish—

things we don't want Him to touch. Since God rarely shouts audibly from the sky, we assume He's pleased with us and go on pursuing our societally approved idolatries. But people who are serious about seeking righteousness refuse to shield any area of life from God's pruning. They also know that God's knife targets some seemingly innocuous things.

I love jazz. When I first became a Christian I owned a sizable record collection. All my discretionary cash went to enlarging my collection. If one of my favorite musicians or bands came out with a new release, I was obsessed with getting it. If I didn't have the money, I would borrow it.

Slowly the Lord began raising questions in my mind as to whether or not even something enjoyable like music should exercise that much control over my desires and behavior. Deciding that it shouldn't, I did the unthinkable. After pulling out a few favorites, I called a friend and said that the rest were his.

Becoming a Christian didn't make me hate jazz. I still love it. I had simply tasted something I wanted more. It was time for a new first love in my life, and my compulsiveness in acquiring jazz albums was starting to slow me down in my pursuit of what I recognized to be far more important. Anything that dulls our spiritual appetite must be restrained or jettisoned. Oswald Chambers said, "Jesus Christ has no tenderness whatever toward anything that is ultimately going to ruin a man in the service of God."[4] Those hot after righteousness know this. They speak these words whole-heartedly with Paul:

> Whatever things were gain to me, those things I have counted as loss for the sake of Christ. More than that, I count all things to be loss in view of the surpassing value of knowing Christ Jesus my Lord, for whom I have suffered the loss of all things, and count them

but rubbish in order that I may gain Christ, and may
be found in Him, not having a righteousness of my
own derived from the Law, but that which is through
faith in Christ, the righteousness which comes from
God on the basis of faith. (Philippians 3:7-9)

People who seek righteousness refuse to be self-
indulgent. They withhold nothing from God. They know
the value of true repentance. It's possible to offer someone
we've offended a pseudo-apology that really doesn't apologize at all. We can say "I'm sorry if I offended you" when we
know full well that we did. Or we can say "I'm sorry but you
must have misunderstood me" when we know very well that
such an "apology" is a lie. The offender isn't sorry. He's
merely going through the motions to save face and cover
pride. And the offended one usually knows it.

Anyone seeking righteousness learns to make apologies without excuses, even when it means losing face or
taking a few lumps—even when it means apologizing for
something in the past. One day as I sat in my office, the
Lord spoke to my heart, telling me to call Fred. Fred was a
pastor I had known for some years. But we had clashed, and
then parted—not exactly as friends. Looking back over the
years and across a few state lines, I knew that both of us
were responsible for the problems between us. But the Lord
told me to call Fred and apologize for my actions and
attitude, for the pain they caused not only him but also his
family. It was clear that God did not want me to mention or
even allude to his part of the blame. I knew that God would
have to be the one to deal with that.

As I dialed the phone I expected to look down to see
my heart bursting through my ribs. As it rang, my hands
shook and fear rose in my chest. But Fred answered, and we
settled things. After I hung up the phone, I felt as if a

long-rooted weed had been torn from my heart.

Stretching in repentance for the righteousness of God's kingdom brings a clean liberation. If apologies aren't enough, restitution may be necessary. When we have stolen or cheated, we need to make it good. When we have broken the law, we should pay the full penalty without using Christianity as a dodge or a plea for leniency. Like Zaccheus (Luke 19:8), we ought to do willingly whatever is needed to set things right.

A fourth trait of those hungering and thirsting after righteousness is a resilient *faith* in the face of adverse circumstances. On many construction jobs, they burn the odd scraps of wood and other materials left over when the job's finished. The Christian wanting to see the character of Christ emerge in his life knows that when God builds, He leaves no scraps. He uses everything, good and bad.

We're not talking about the kind of easy-believism that expects God to do everything. Nor is this a fatalism, which wrings its hands and moans that everything is God's will. People who have that kind of mindset will probably feel pain and confusion over their circumstances. But those who seek righteousness will be confident that God can be trusted to use absolutely anything to draw them closer to Him, to fit them for His likeness and service.

> How does God in grace prosecute this purpose? Not by shielding us from assault by the world, the flesh, and the devil, nor by protecting us from burdensome and frustrating circumstances, nor yet by shielding us from troubles created by our own temperament and psychology; but rather by exposing us to all these things, so as to overwhelm us with a sense of our own inadequacy, and to drive us to cling to Him more closely.[5]

Boxers in training will often let their sparring partners hit them repeatedly in the chest and stomach. They feel that it helps toughen them. Whether it does or not, the Christian can respond in the same way to things like harsh criticism and slander.

George Whitefield, the great preacher, never lived under anything but a hailstorm of attack. Slander in the press from clergy and nobles and from every imaginable direction assailed him until he died. But George Whitefield never retaliated in kind. He chose to use the slander as an exercise in deflating his pride, a curb on his appetite for the praise of men.

We can make the same intentional response to most things that come our way. Living like that puts a strong brake on complaining and whining, chronic symptoms of a fallen nature that must get the last word in every situation.

THE URGE TO FORGIVE

Forgiveness does not come easily to many. To be right, to be vindicated, to get revenge, is far more palatable. That's why Jesus is clearly describing a kingdom appetite when He says, "Blessed are the merciful, for they shall receive mercy" (Matthew 5:7).

But something deep inside of us cries out in protest at these words of Jesus. We manage to choke down the other beatitudes, but this is almost too much. Yet other scriptures hem us in even tighter: "If you forgive men for their transgressions, your heavenly Father will also forgive you. But if you do not forgive men, then your Father will not forgive your transgressions" (Matthew 6:14-15).

Doesn't God know the pain some people have inflicted? Doesn't He know what monsters they were? And by withholding His forgiveness if I withhold mine, isn't God using

His muscle as leverage to extract an insincere forgiveness from me just so I can receive an act of forgiveness I really need?

The point is not what God knows but what we've forgotten. Jesus helps us remember in His parable of the kingdom in Matthew 18:21-35. It seems that a servant was in debt to his master for ten thousand talents (the equivalent of several million dollars in silver). Since the servant couldn't pay, his master proceeded to sell the servant and his family to recoup part of the debt. But the servant begged and pleaded. Moved with great compassion, the master not only released the man but completely forgave the debt.

Later this same servant ran across one of his buddies who owed him about a day's wage. He grabbed this fellow around the neck and throttled him, demanding to be paid. When this second servant begged for mercy, using the same words the first servant used with his master, it was useless. The second servant was thrown into debtor's prison until he could pay. Word of what happened reached the ears of the master and he angrily confronted the first slave:

> "His lord said to him, 'You wicked slave, I forgave you all that debt because you entreated me. Should you not also have had mercy on your fellow slave, even as I had mercy on you?' And his lord, moved with anger, handed him over to the torturers until he should repay all that was owed him. So shall My heavenly Father also do to you, if each of you does not forgive his brother from your heart." (Matthew 18:32-35)

We are so quick to forget the sheer magnitude of what God has forgiven us. Maybe we've never really considered the extent of God's forgiveness. But when we indulge hate or attempt to justify a grudge, we're like that servant who was forgiven a huge debt only to turn around and nail someone for a comparatively little sum. Notice I said comparatively. I would never want to demean the serious pain I see in others' lives—pain suffered at the hands of others.

But we must keep the perspective of this parable. No matter what someone has done to me, only my sin is serious enough to render me guilty of judgment and hell. No one else's sin can have that effect in my life. Jesus Christ wasn't killed by cowardly or traitorous disciples, power-mad religious leaders, ambivalent political leaders, fickle crowds, or calloused soldiers. You and I killed Christ; our sin put Him on that Roman cross. One of the murderers of the Son of God is writing these words. Another is reading them. And God forgave it all.

Christian forgiveness is not slapping a superficial, thin veneer of piety on top of a layer of seething anger for a wrong suffered. It's not a phony spiritual giddiness trying to mask the pain of ripped-up insides. Christian forgiveness is an act of the will where we look at the sin of those who wound us the way *God* sees it. He sees our sin and the sin of our offender both in the shadow of the Cross.

When we are reminded of how much we've been forgiven, our heart should soften enough to forgive others. This is a highly delicate matter orchestrated by the Holy Spirit. It's highly problematic, even presumptuous, for someone to go to another in deep pain, wave Scripture under his nose, and then demand unequivocally that he forgive those who have crushed him. God's Spirit alone knows when to raise the issue. When he does, those whose hearts live under the Cross and seek the kingdom of God stand predisposed to be merciful because they know full well how much they have been forgiven. "Be kind to one another, tender-hearted, forgiving each other, just as God in Christ also has forgiven you" (Ephesians 4:32).

God is not being cruel when He refuses to forgive us if we refuse to forgive others. Something hard and thick comes over the soul of a person who will never forgive.

> Of the Seven Deadly Sins, anger is possibly the most fun. To lick your wounds, to smack your lips over grievances long past, to roll over your tongue the prospect of bitter confrontations still to come, to savor the last toothsome morsel of both the pain you are given and the pain you are giving back—in many ways it is a feast fit for a king. The chief drawback is that what you are wolfing down is yourself. The skeleton at the feast is you.[6]

This black hardness polarizes us away from repentance since our choosing to dwell on the sin of another renders us blind and indulgent toward our own. A heart without repentance God cannot and will not forgive.

When Christians are merciful toward others as God is, it always stops people in their tracks. The turn of the century was a dangerous time to be in China. In 1900, the Boxer Rebellion erupted and rumors of missionaries and Chinese Christians being slaughtered were widespread. Almost a hundred missionaries and their families had been murdered in Shansi Province on the orders of the governor himself.

As the violence finally subsided, James Graham traveled north to see if it was safe for missionaries to return. While he was there, Graham received a visitor late one night—a hard, cruel looking man. Graham was astonished to learn that this man presided over the execution at Shansi where many of those killed had been Graham's friends. The executioner had been deeply shaken by men, women, and children dying while singing the praises of Jesus. He knew by the way they died that this Jesus must truly be God. "But," he said, "tell me. Can God forgive my so-great sin? ... Is there nothing, nothing I might do to atone for my wrong? Is there nothing?"

Graham had choked down his boiling rage and indignation all through this incredible story. He thought of dear friends dying at this man's hands. Yet he found himself strangely saying, "Our God, whom we serve, is a merciful God. True, your sin was great. Very great. But His mercy is even greater. This Jesus is His Son, who came to earth to die for sinners like you. I, too, am a sinner. All men are sinners. And because He died for you, for Jesus His Son's sake, God can forgive you."[7] That night a missionary stood together in the shadow of the Cross with the murderer of his closest friends and brought him to Christ. Christian forgiveness is one of the most effective sermons many will hear.

THE APPETITE FOR A CLEAR, CLEAN LIFE

A friend of mine raises pigs. One day we went to the barn to see the latest batch of piglets. About forty quivering snouts and sets of little pink eyes turned to greet us. A large lamp burned over the pen to help keep them warm. But sometimes the light would go out. With the light out, the temperature in an unheated barn on a cool night can drop to life-threatening levels.

One morning he came in to find thirty piglets stretched out cold, seemingly dead. Immediately his wife filled five gallon buckets with warm water, and holding these cold stiff piglets so that just the nose broke the surface, they submerged the lifeless animals in the water. Some didn't make it. But some began to regain color and warmth. They jerked and twitched and acted like we would if we'd awakened to find ourselves held under water by our nose!

Becoming a Christian means more than being freed from the penalty of our past sin, even though it certainly includes that. It means more than having Christ solve our problems, although in numerous cases it surely means that. As in the case of the piglets, there is an infusion of new life. For them it was a re-animation of life that was almost lost. For us it's an infusion of the life of God. We begin to taste a cleanness, an inner quality of the heart. Tasting some should only make us want more.

Jesus referred to this appetite when He said, "Blessed are the pure in heart, for they shall see God" (Matthew 5:8). This kind of purity has two sides to it. One is holiness. The average person who doesn't know Christ doesn't care about holiness. The one who has the life of Christ imparted to his heart through the Holy Spirit should grow to care of little else. His heart-cry is the prayer of the Scotsman Robert Murray MCheyne, who said, "Lord, make me as holy as a saved sinner can be." Some might think this desire odd. But those who have developed this gnawing appetite for holiness in their pursuit of the kingdom of God are oblivious to outside opinions.

That brings us to purity's other side—the idea of being undivided or unmixed. One man describes this as "the single-minded, who are free from the tyranny of a divided self."[8] Most of us live at the mercy of important but segmented concerns. The job, the family, the house, and a dozen other things put us through our paces like a circus clown juggling plates. While three or four things may be spinning well, one could crash to the ground any minute.

Purity here describes the sublimation of all these pressing things to the desire to live solely for the glory of God. Moreover, it describes the integration of these things as well. A major reason why these dimensions of life can take as big a bite of us as they do is that they have become far too important. But the pure in heart see with a single eye (Matthew 6:22). Their desire to live for God's glory and God's kingdom order the legitimate concerns of life like the spokes of a wheel around the hub.

One day a friend named Cheryl walked up to me and I didn't recognize her. In many ways, her life had been a nightmare. Now as I looked at her in happy surprise, it was hard to believe this was the same woman. Her marriage had stabilized and her children were fine. She was almost finished with nursing school. Even the haggard features and sunken eyes were gone. Anyone meeting Cheryl now would never guess what her life had been. What once had been a shattered life was now a complete life with direction. There had been a restoration of, not naiveté, but genuine innocence.

What had brought about this change? Jesus Christ had made her pure in heart. The frayed threads of her life were now entwined to make a strong cord. Such a binding force brings great clarity to life. It also brings a spontaneous unpretentiousness like a breath of fresh air. A new appetite grows within, rising from the hearts of those seeking first the kingdom of God.

DESIRING HONEST PEACE

Ours is a bloody planet. Our history is one long case study on conflict at every level of existence. Peace has been an elusive thing. Not merely a problem of international scope, conflict has sifted down to the personal level as human relationships lie in fractured bits and pieces. The world needs peacemakers—not people with ideals and good intentions, but people who can make a difference. Where can they be found?

Seeking the kingdom of God is never a quest merely to

become spiritual. It means that as our relationship with God deepens, our nature becomes conformed to Christ's nature as we set our hearts on what God desires to bring about in the world. With that in mind, it should come as no surprise that Jesus should say, "Blessed are the peacemakers, for they shall be called sons of God" (Matthew 5:9).

The quest for peace does not begin at the bargaining table; it must begin individually in every human heart. Marchers demonstrating for world peace, who do not take into account the sinful nature of man, often show a naiveté that makes it difficult to take them seriously. As sin destroys the peace of individual lives, families, neighborhoods, and communities, the peace between nations will surely suffer repeated breakdowns.

Evangelism is not peripheral to world peace. It wages the battle for peace where it really counts. Paul wrote, "Therefore having been justified by faith, we have peace with God through our Lord Jesus Christ" (Romans 5:1). Coming to Christ means that the state of hostility between God and us has ceased. The rebels have unconditionally surrendered. It's no coincidence that the gospel has brought peace between man and man, just as it brings peace between God and man.

Peace with God is more than just a spiritual cease-fire. It's a living quality at the core of our heart that is not at the mercy of fluctuating emotions. It is based on our faith in the truth of the gospel instead of external circumstances (John 14:27). True peace with God spurs us on with a courage not our own when the concerns of His kingdom are in jeopardy (John 16:33). It stands ready to defend the heart and mind against all onslaughts of doubt and fear (Philippians 4:7). It is living evidence of the Holy Spirit's presence (Galatians 5:22).

The peace of God must be seen in the church in order

to be credible. It only follows that the world should see something uniquely peaceful when the people of God gather as the church. In the introduction to every letter he wrote, whether to churches or to individuals, Paul wished them grace and peace. The contemporary church, while it should be a showcase for both grace and peace, often shows by its behavior that it knows little of either. That's the risk when sinners, even redeemed ones, gather together.

But the church is ideally the place where all the natural enmities that divide men simply do not count (Ephesians 2:13-15). Christians are to go to extremes to be at peace with one another and to maintain an honest Spirit-controlled unity in the church (Romans 14:19, Ephesians 4:3). Getting our way or squabbling over minor issues is never the main issue. Yet sometimes separation is necessary. Nevertheless, most church splits are sinful. And the few that may not be sinful still discredit the gospel of peace.

When Paul directed leaders at Philippi to reunite two alienated leaders (Philippians 4:2-3), there was more at stake than just their friendship. Listen to Francis Schaeffer:

> I have observed one thing among true Christians in their differences in many countries: what divides and severs true Christian groups and Christians—what leaves a bitterness that can last for 20, 30, or 40 years (or for 50 or 60 years in a son's memory)—is not the issue of doctrine or belief which caused the differences in the first place. Invariably it is lack of love—and the bitter things that are said; by true Christians in the midst of differences. These stick in the mind like glue. And after time passes and the differences between the Christians or the groups appear less than they did, there are still those bitter, bitter things we said in the midst of what we thought was a good and

sufficient objective discussion. It is these things—
these unloving attitudes and words—that cause the
stench that the world can smell in the church of Jesus
Christ among those who are really true Christians.[9]

Peace keeping is costly business. All the beatitudes
mentioned before should be in strong evidence. "There
will be the pain of listening, of ridding ourselves of prejudice, of striving sympathetically to understand both the
opposing points of view, and of risking misunderstanding,
ingratitude or failure."[10]

The world needs peace in every corner, at every level
of existence. Some of our best efforts at peace have gone
sour. The League of Nations failed. The United Nations,
while it hasn't failed, has hardly been an unqualified success. Nothing has really changed. Men are still lovers of self.
We still hear of wars and rumors of wars. Modern peacemakers are often dwarfed by the magnitude of the problem,
intimidated because of the inadequacy of their resources or
governed by self-interest. Today Christianity has a tremendous opportunity to show the world a group of people
who have something rising from deep within—which cannot be explained in human terms—that makes men love
when they would by nature hate.

Billy McCurrie's dad was gunned down by IRA terror-
ists in Belfast when he was twelve. Billy became obsessed
with avenging his father's death and joined a Protestant
paramilitary group. Of those days he says, "I would have
had no qualms in shooting or blowing up anybody."[11] One
night he killed a suspected informer in the group and was
imprisoned as a convicted murderer. He was only seventeen.

While in prison he studied every religion and philosophy known to man. Through Christian prisoners, guards,
and a woman working inside the prison, Billy McCurrie

found the life-transforming power of Jesus Christ. Now Billy is out of prison and preparing for the ministry—perhaps a jail ministry. He plans to spend the rest of his life in Northern Ireland showing Protestants and Catholics alike the power of the gospel of Jesus Christ that can cleanse a man of hate and all sin from the inside out. God has the same task in mind for us wherever we live—bringing love from out of the ashes of hate. But will we run the risk of doing it?

A DOUBLE BLESSING BADLY NEEDED

Someone once said that a pastor should have the heart of a child and the hide of a rhinoceros. These are important traits for *all* who seek the kingdom of God. When we come to know Christ we're not always ready for the responses we get. Some of us get caught flatfooted when others don't share the enthusiasm for Christ and His kingdom that we have.

The initial shock of opposition or disapproval can hobble Christians young and old. That is why one of the clearest notes in the New Testament is that of persecution. We're plainly told that "all who desire to live godly in Christ Jesus will be persecuted" (2 Timothy 3:12). All aspirants to God's kingdom are told right at the beginning what to expect. Jesus Christ never draws anyone to Himself under pretense. But Christ not only warns; He keenly notices when His own suffer the consequences of following Him:

> "Blessed are those who have been persecuted for the sake of righteousness, for theirs is the kingdom of heaven. Blessed are you when men cast insults at you, and persecute you, and say all kinds of evil against you falsely, on account of Me. Rejoice, and

be glad, for your reward in heaven is great, for so
they persecuted the prophets who were before you."
(Matthew 5:10-12)

This persecution is unique. We expect hostility when
we offend, wound, or violate someone. But this is hostility
that will arise spontaneously in our lives when we've not
brought it on ourselves. Jesus' own words tell us this will
happen for two reasons. One is for righteousness' sake.
People who hunger and thirst for righteousness also draw
critics and make enemies. Don't all of us feel resentful
against those who make us look bad? A hard worker embar-
rasses a lazy one just by example. One person seeking righteousness has such a sensitivity to sin that by sheer force of
living he will show up those who do not share his quest.

A person who truly seeks righteousness will fight for
justice, championing any number of unpopular causes,
thereby pricking the conscience of the status quo. The usual
deterrents don't stop him because these deterrents all aim
at temporal securities or play on temporal fears.

Much of the German church capitulated to Hitler's
government in the 1930s. They became pawns of a corrupt
state. But some voices would not mouth party lies and
refused to be silent. Paul Schneider fearlessly preached that
Christ alone was Lord. Warned by the Gestapo that his
children could become orphans if he refused to stop, he
said, "Better that they should be orphans than grow up and
know that their father bowed down to the devil instead of to
the living God."[12] Paul Schneider died in Buchenwald,
where his voice could be heard raised against evil even
from the cells of solitary confinement.

Those who are hot after righteousness cannot be
intimidated or bought off. Their lives are signposts and
their voices megaphones for the God they love and whose

kingdom they seek.

The second reason for this persecution is simply because of Christ. The world hates Him. It will hate all who genuinely follow Him: "If the world hates you, you know that it has hated Me before it hated you" (John 15:18).

We live in a pluralistic age where the options are open and relatively equal. The final determinant is the spiritual palate of the individual. Jesus Christ has been misrepresented as one among many other gurus, wizards, masters, or ways. He is not. He alone is God, Savior, and Lord. Everyone must come to Him on His terms alone, or else face judgment and hell.

In the eyes of the world, these are harsh terms, and so they are unpopular. Anyone who in any way is a reminder of Christ and His unalterable claims will know persecution. He will sometimes be slandered and will feel the alienation of others.

We must steel ourselves here. Most of us aren't confrontational types. We like being liked. Somehow this desire for popularity has become ingrained into the ecclesiastical woodwork so that Christian witness has come to mean being a nice bunch of people who never offend anyone. Jesus said, "Woe to you when all men speak well of you" (Luke 6:26). The praise of all men is not the fruit of witness but of cowardice and betrayal. We must all beware of compromise. For when the complimentary words of the world become our meat and drink, we are in danger of forgetting our primary mission.

The people in the early church received tremendous opposition from all sides. Today we see the same tendency toward persecution in many settings. The more momentum for the kingdom of God a life or ministry gains, the more the opposition and persecution increase as well. We should expect it. We should also not be blinded to the benefits of persecution. Suffering for the kingdom of God makes us part of a great company. Even when no one around us may understand, there is a great cloud of witnesses who have suffered and gone before us (Hebrews 12:1). Deep in our spirits we are understood and not alone.

Persecution also makes us strong. It is a strong tree that grows leaning into the wind. It's no coincidence that the churches in many poor and oppressed countries show a maturity and toughness not seen in Western churches. After a lengthy visit to the United States, Helmut Thielicke, German pastor and theologian, was asked what he saw as the greatest defect among American Christians. He said, "They have an inadequate view of suffering."[13]

Finally, persecution provides the greatest assurance that we really do belong to Christ:

> Beloved, do not be surprised at the fiery ordeal among you, which comes upon you for your testing, as though some strange thing were happening to you; but to the degree that you share the sufferings of Christ, keep on rejoicing; so that also at the revelation of His glory, you may rejoice with exultation. If you are reviled for the name of Christ, you are blessed, because the Spirit of glory and of God rests upon you. By no means let any of you suffer as a murderer, or thief, or evildoer, or a troublesome meddler; but if anyone suffers as a Christian, let him not feel ashamed, but in that name let him glorify God.
> (1 Peter 4:12-16)

Richard Wurmbrand, a pastor imprisoned behind the Iron Curtain, was tortured and put in solitary confinement. Although weak and in pain, he felt such a joy at the presence of Christ in his cell that he literally jumped and danced. That's exactly what Christ said to do. "Rejoice, and be glad." For those who won't be turned away by persecution or opposition from seeking His kingdom, God has the highest possible honor. Their quest will be fulfilled; they will receive His kingdom and much more.

My college roommate, Bob, and I once told another student about Christ. Although I don't think we did anything to offend him, he became angry and called us everything he could think of. As we left the dorm, Bob turned to me and said, "Dave, I'm glad you were with me today. We just had a great experience."

I thought, *What room were* you *in?* But Bob was right. He was on to something. When others treat us the way Jesus was treated, it's a sign that we're headed in the right direction. To be lifted out of ourselves and be used by God to point others toward Him is joy unspeakable. Should we happen to be mistreated, it's incidental: "For I consider that the sufferings of this present time are not worthy to be compared with the glory that is to be revealed to us" (Romans 8:18). The man who wrote that knew what it was to sing praises to God in the night while locked in the shackles of a Roman prison. A couple of his buddies took a beating because they refused to stop preaching Christ. When they were released, they walked off rejoicing. Because they were released? No. It was because they were found worthy to suffer for His name (Acts 5:41)!

These three men were on to something, too—something that rises only in the heart of someone who feels compelled to pursue the kingdom of God. The world is dying. Jesus Christ can transform it. The two must be brought together. How we are treated in the process is of little significance. As we grow new appetites for eternal rewards, we will in no way be disappointed—no matter what the opposition or the cost.

8
The Agenda of Another World

—◆—

The people had paid plenty to attend this government inaugural. Power—raw political power—rippled through the room as people with nationally known faces and reputations took their seats. The emcee introduced a clergyman who was to give the invocation. As the man approached the rostrum, the room fell silent, conversation trailed off, and heads bowed.

What started as a prayer took some unusual twists. There were two or three jokes, and even a quote from Yogi Berra's farewell speech at Yankee Stadium. A good-humored political slap at the newly elected official's opponents, as well as a plethora of praises for the official herself, rounded things off. When they were first told that they were going to pray, the tuxedoed politicians and their wives seemed visibly uncomfortable. But as the prayer turned out to be the type of banter they themselves used in campaigning and public speaking, they soon raised their heads and laughed along with the rest. A hearty round of applause followed the "amen." When prayer is used as a front for a joke—strutting and preening before an audience of men instead of humbly coming before the audience of God—something is very wrong in the heart of the one who "prays."

While we have no right to sit in judgment on the legitimate prayers of others, we'd do well to listen to ourselves. We say a lot about how well we know God by what we ask for and how we ask. People who are seeking the kingdom of God pray differently than the fickle masses who seek God only in times of trouble and forget Him when that trouble passes. True believers show that their heart can see into eternity. And so they press on for the achievement of the weightiest items on the heart of God in the only way these can be attained. They pray with an authenticity of heart that both moves God and melts men.

Jesus left us a model of prayer in Matthew 6:9-13. We know it as the Lord's Prayer. Many can say it by heart. It takes only seconds. But it is quite a different thing to say it from the heart. To do so will take us on a more costly route through an entire lifetime of smashing down obstacles to His kingdom until all creation bows at the feet of Christ. The world does not applaud this kind of prayer.

Prayer is an extraordinary thing. In biblical times one entered the presence of an oriental potentate at his own peril. To come unbidden meant certain death. (See Esther 4:11 for an example.) Only if the king was gracious could the petitioner come safely. On a higher level, the priest could enter the Holy of Holies in both the Tabernacle and the Temple only on the Day of Atonement. But when Christ died, the massive veil of the Temple was ripped down the middle, symbolizing that through Christ's death all could go freely, even boldly into the presence of God.

> Since therefore, brethren, we have confidence to enter the holy place by the blood of Jesus, by a new and living way which He inaugurated for us through

the veil, that is, His flesh, and since we have a great
priest over the house of God, let us draw near with a
sincere heart in full assurance of faith, having our
hearts sprinkled clean from an evil conscience and
our bodies washed with pure water. (Hebrews 10:19-22)

Now in prayer we come to One greater than any
earthly potentate. Whenever there is need we come before
One whom men cannot look upon and live. And beyond
that, we're encouraged to do so with the unprecedented
familial name *Father* on our lips: "Our Father who art in
heaven." That we can address the Creator of the universe
with such an intimate name and actually bring deep joy to
our Father's heart is astounding. If we've never been struck
dumb with astonishment at this, a big piece of our spiritual
education is missing.

> If you want to judge how well a person understands
> Christianity, find out how much he makes of the
> thought of being God's child, and having God as his
> Father. If this is not the thought that prompts and
> controls his worship and prayers and his whole out-
> look on life, it means that he does not understand
> Christianity very well at all.[1]

To pray "Our Father who art in heaven" as Jesus bids
us to do is an incredible privilege. People who are truly
seeking His kingdom take these words on their lips
prostrate—if not bodily (although this would be appropriate), certainly in heart. The prayer we will now examine
has been painted on wall plaques, stitched into tea towels,
and even engraved on pennies. But if this prayer doesn't
rise like incense smoke from our hearts, then it hasn't been
written in the one place for which it was intended.

FIRST THINGS FIRST

We do a terrible, almost blasphemous thing in prayer. We invert the agenda, putting *our* concerns at the top of the list and somehow never quite getting to *God's* concerns. Jesus, in giving us these words, did not intend to merely give us something profound to quote. His prayer is a model for all Christians whenever they pray. It is the agenda as it has been fixed in heaven. This is the primary docket of God's concern. It was given us to follow, not to revise.

We need to listen to our typical prayers. If we are ruthlessly honest we'll discover some revealing things about our relationship with God. Perhaps many of our prayers are caught up in some way with daily bread, forgiveness, deliverance from temptation, and protection from the Evil One. Okay, that's good. But while we should pray about these things, they can become consumptive. When we never get farther than praying for sicknesses and surgeries, protection when we travel, help in paying bills, and that kind of thing, something is missing. God never hears from some of us unless we want something. When do things of first priority with God ever come up?

The first thing that needs to surface in our lives is the hallowing of God's name. What does that mean? Culturally names mean little to us, serving only as identification labels. But names in biblical times served a vital purpose. They described the nature or essence of their possessor.

> In the tradition of the Orient, a name is not merely a vocable having its own distinct sound and letters, but expresses the inner nature of its intended object. The ancient biblical world recognized an inner relationship between reality and language, and particularly between name and character. The name not only

serves the purpose of identification . . . but also serves
as a descriptive and definitive function in the disclo-
sure of the inner nature. . . . The name penetrates to
the inner secret of one's nature and discloses what is
hidden from mere external knowledge.[2]

God's name is to be hallowed because it tells us of His
character. It discloses to us the divine nature. We're also
called to hallow God's name because it is special knowledge
that no man can attain on his own. We know God because
He chose to make Himself known. He did not have to, and
had He not done so we would be powerless to know Him.
Our best efforts would be vain speculation.

Revelation occurs because God wills it to occur. Man
does not control the process. He cannot decide that
he will embark on such and such a process in the sure
knowledge that in the end he will compel God to
speak. God speaks when and as He chooses. God is
not committed to man or to any place or any way of
revealing Himself to man.[3]

The one who hallows God's name longs to know,
adore, and serve the only true God. We live in an ostenta-
tious, yet shriveled age when men hallow very little. The
jaded sophistication that characterizes the world has seeped
into the church. That the name of God has become nothing
more than an empty epithet to the world should not surprise us. But it should break our hearts. It's the primary
business of those who seek the kingdom of God both in
prayer and action to not only make His name known but to
want others to hallow, honor, and worship it as they do.
  Hard on the heels of the desire to hallow God's name
come the desires that His kingdom would come and that

His will be done on earth as it is in heaven. While the kingdom of God was inaugurated through the life and ministry of Jesus Christ, it is still incomplete. God's will is openly flaunted. A cursory glance at the newspaper provides ample evidence of both.

One night the light was on late in William Booth's home. Fearing his father ill, Bramwell, his son, went next door and found his father pacing. Dressed in an old nightshirt and with a wet towel coiled around his head to stave off a splitting headache, Booth stopped to look at his son. "Ought you not to be asleep?" Bramwell asked.

"No, I am thinking," William replied. Seeing the puzzlement on his son's face, he walked over and placed his hands on his son's shoulders. "Bramwell," he said, "I am thinking about the people's sins. What will they do with their sins?"[4]

Indeed, what will happen to the people who do not hallow the name of God, who care nothing for His kingdom or His will? William Booth knew, and so do all who seek God's kingdom. Those outside the kingdom will perish.

As we come to ponder the fact that millions perish and that humanity lies broken and crushed under every kind of injustice, the awful weight of this knowledge becomes a constant companion. The world might ask why we are borrowing trouble. We must say that we know God because He has made Himself known to us, and that we know the reality of the world to be death. As one writer has described it, God has hung a CONDEMNED sign over our planet. We can accept no lasting ease while men who are blind to God's glory in this dying relic of a world live as if it were a palace.

HEALING ON THE WAY

We must face squarely several implications of seeing into eternity as do people who pray this way. First, to always put our need in front of God's priorities is idolatry. The key word is *always*. It's certainly right to pray for daily bread, especially when the table is bare. It's right to ask for the forgiveness of our sins. It's right to pray for loved ones as they're wheeled into surgery, or for protection as our headlights show nothing but a glare of ice on the road ahead. But for some people this is all there is.

Christ (as well as His church) never hears from certain people unless they want something. Is God really nothing more than a means to our ends? Is it His main goal to get our needs met, help us feel good about ourselves, get our marriage, kids, or sexuality straightened out, and keep our careers on track? To never pray beyond these concerns is to demand that God bow His knee at the altar of our need, that He subjugate His concerns to ours. People in all kinds of pain or affliction may fixate on their need. But we must never expect God to do so.

I don't want to seem insensitive to anyone's pain. There are indeed times when it's overwhelming. Please notice, however, that there is no exemption clause to seeking first the kingdom of God. We're not told in Scripture to pull things together first. Some part of our lives will *always* be under construction. It is common for people in pain to turn inward. But if that inwardness is not tempered by some form of reaching out, the pain is often prolonged and sometimes more deeply ingrained. The most hurting Christians should be encouraged to find just one corner of their lives where they can lose themselves for God's kingdom.

For much of her life, Connie had had a terrible fear of water. Just being in a swimming pool, let alone learning to swim, was a horrifying experience. Even riding on bridges over water put a knot of terror in her stomach. The root of her fear was a relationship from early adolescence. One winter, she and a boyfriend got into an argument. He stalked angrily away to go ice fishing with his brother. His anger led him to be careless. As a result he fell through the ice and drowned.

From the day of his death, Connie was gripped by this compulsive fear of water. She blamed herself for her boyfriend's death. Then one day the opportunity came to be a camp counselor. Connie loved Christ and young people. She also had a great heart for missions. There was only one thing holding her back. The camp had a swimming pool. And there was boating on the river. She knew she'd have to participate if she wanted to be effective with the girls there.

Connie could have decided she wasn't ready to face this challenge. But she longed to see Christ do something great in the lives of these girls, and so she came to camp. The day came when we were to go canoeing. In cabin devotions the night before, God gave Connie a word just for her. She shared that message and her story with the girls. The scripture was Isaiah 43:1-2: "Do not fear, for I have redeemed you; I have called you by name; you are Mine! When you pass through the waters, I will be with you; and through the rivers, they will not overflow you." Not only did Connie go canoeing without incident, but her terrible bondage to fear and guilt was broken. She is free to this day.

Rita is a woman who taught our Sunday school class. At one time she must have been a beautiful woman. Complications from a heart problem had ravaged her health. Her skin was pale and drawn, her hair brittle. Rita suffered from all this for many years. A second crushing blow came when her husband left her with two adolescent sons for another woman. How strong the desire must have been to curl up and withdraw. But Rita loved Christ and sought His kingdom.

Being in Rita's class was a joy not to be missed. She was neither a stoic nor a glutton for pity. She never tried to hide her pain or wallow in it. There were Sundays when life got the better of her emotionally, but she was still at her desk, even when the wind chill hit fifty below. Her class drew wounded people who otherwise would never have entered a church. A parade of these people passed through her home as well.

Both Connie and Rita had been mauled by life. Although a thousand well-intentioned voices would have shouted to be concerned with daily bread and protection from the Evil One, these two women had already made a prior commitment to follow one Voice, which urged them to hallow His name. Their goal was to seek to advance His kingdom and to obey His will. Putting His concerns first, they both found substantial healing along the way.

THE NEED TO SERVE

A second implication of putting God's concerns first should lead us to rethink our theology of church membership. A Norwegian student and I sat discussing the differences between American and European Christianity. "You Americans," he said, "are very practical. You are masters of technique and method—always looking for a better way of doing something. But you are shallow in your theology of almost everything."

After I choked down my defensiveness, I had to agree. We want better, faster, more convenient ways of doing things, but don't ask us why we're doing those things in the first place.

Much of church membership today is caught firmly in the grip of a consumer mindset. People look for a church based on the range of services and amenities offered. While families all have legitimate needs to be met, we've come to view church membership largely in terms of what we can get out of it. And churches are responding in kind by treating people as consumers. The church down the street becomes the competition. Pastors and leaders find themselves aping salesmen as they visit homes trying to convince a family that their programs are just the thing this family is looking for.

Churches need to stop prostituting their calling. They should be whatever Christ wants them to be. If that doesn't meet a certain visitor's need, then those people should look for another church. Some may find this hard to swallow, but it is not God's will for everyone to join our church.

The local church is an expression of the Body of Christ. Paul is very clear as to the criteria employed by the Holy Spirit in putting it together:

> One and the same Spirit works all these things, distributing to each one individually just as He wills. For even as the body is one and yet has many members, and all the members of the body, though they are many, are one body, so also is Christ. For by one Spirit we were all baptized into one body, whether Jews or Greeks, whether slaves or free, and we were all made to drink of one Spirit. . . . But now God has placed the members, each one of them, in the body, just as He desired. (1 Corinthians 12:11-13,18)

People who seek God's kingdom and pray, putting God's concerns first, know that the primary reason they are in a certain church is that God has placed them there so that their gifts can mesh with those of others to form a coordinated spiritual body reaching out to society.

The music program may not be what it was in the last church. The youth group may leave something to be desired. The will of God simply isn't always cut from the mold of our expectations or perceived needs. Suzie may not need a youth choir that tours every summer wearing color coordinated shirts. Mom may not really need a women's group that luncheons frequently.

A new work in a nearby town was off to a terrible start. The nucleus proved fickle and evaporated soon after the new pastor arrived. Subsequent visiting and canvassing yielded meager results. On many Sundays the pastor had no one to preach to other than his wife.

A man named Phil lived in another town and learned of the struggling church. Phil belonged to a church that wasn't large but had all the basic ministries a family could want. After prayerful thought, Phil and his family joined the struggling little church and immediately volunteered to serve in numerous positions. They also spent several Saturdays visiting in the community. The new congregation began to take hold.

Phil could have found legitimate support for his desire to stay in an established church. However, for Phil and his family, hallowing God's name, seeking His kingdom, and doing His will took them in other directions. Why would someone who claims to love Christ want to lie buried in a church doing nothing except sitting on the receiving end of someone else's ministry?

Any given church has more ministry than its currently active members can do. Some churches are in desperate straits and need help immediately. What a worthy challenge—to join the smallest, most struggling church we can find and then bury ourselves in it for the glory of Christ and His kingdom. Those in the church who are myopically fixated on their own needs might ponder a need that is often ignored—the need to serve. And the next time we say the Lord's Prayer, we might ask ourselves if we've been living in only the last half of it.

VICTORY—WHEN GOD WINS

A third implication of putting God's concerns first involves a hard look at Christian victory. Biblically and historically, victory in Christ has meant that Christ's cause and kingdom are advanced. Personal consequences or well-being have been subjugated to this overriding concern.

Today we have become fuzzy as to the process and nature of Christian victory. Victory presupposes battle or struggle. While Christians through the ages have known struggle to be a valuable part of the spiritual apparatus, today that is not so. Struggle and conflict are to be avoided. Spirituality should bring peace and comfort.

We have trouble relating to the great spiritual wrestling recorded in both Scripture and in history. We resist the scriptural message that conflict and pain are not something to be avoided or just endured but something to be actively engaged in. It is simply part of the business of growing in Christ. It's no coincidence that most Christian "testimonies" are retroactive, going back many years. When Christianity is lived in a way that eschews struggle, there are few current victories to show.

Too often we recognize victory only when our concerns turn out well, when we look good. I will never forget one man I met at a men's breakfast. The man had worry and fear scrawled on his face and I soon learned why. He'd made major mistakes in some business ventures and in some investments. He was within a couple of days of complete financial ruin if things didn't change. Someone had brought him as a new Christian to this meeting, and almost everyone was backslapping and giving glib reassurances that God would bring victory. Scripture promising prosperity was quoted freely. Three days later everything fell apart and the man lost everything.

When we talked later, he said he was fighting to save his house. It was impossible to miss his bitterness over a victory others had promised that never materialized. It wasn't his fault. He'd been set up by well-intentioned friends who recognized Christian victory only when their problems were solved. No wonder many people are largely unable to comprehend the lack of preoccupation with self in Scripture and history.

What about all the believers throughout the course of history who were beat up, persecuted, and even killed for their faith? (Hebrews 11 tells their stories well.) Would we see their experiences as victory? They were. The good news was preached to the lost, and the grace of God was held out to people without hope. God considers their living commitment an unqualified success. What about the suffering of all these believers? Strictly an occupational hazard when you seek first God's kingdom.

A CHURCH WITH KINGDOM EYES

Scripture gives us a look at a tremendous cross section of a church full of people who put God's concerns first. That praying church in Acts 4 backed Peter and John's ministry, even in the midst of their imprisonment. This was a church that surely had the Lord's Prayer written on the people's hearts. Some would have seen victory in Peter and John's release from prison and stopped there. Not these people. While we might pray for protection, they sought boldness and power to do more of what had already gotten them into trouble—only with more intensity.

> "And now, Lord, take note of their threats, and grant that Thy bond-servants may speak Thy word with all confidence, while Thou dost extend Thy hand to

heal, and signs and wonders take place through the name of Thy holy servant Jesus." (Acts 4:29-30)

How did God answer? The place where they prayed was shaken with a mighty outpouring of the Holy Spirit. Many today claim supernatural experiences. There are many more who have had them and remained silent. As it is the sin of unbelief to worship spiritual experiences or to deny them, this passage provides needed insight.

First, the thinking and thus the praying was grounded in the Word of God. Scripture is foundational for all of Christian living. Spiritual experience can be intoxicating, and those who have overwhelming experiences must always fight the temptation to make those experiences normative and Scripture merely supportive.

Second, these people in the early church were not seeking an experience. Even their request for power to work signs and wonders wasn't so that they could spiritually gloat over what they did. The experience came by God's grace. All godly experiences do. We foolishly assume that someone's spiritual experience marks him as being mature. Often it indicates quite the opposite. The desire to perform signs and wonders was really a desire to focus the world's attention on Christ and His gospel.

Third, those early Christians did not spend this experience on themselves. The Holy Spirit is never poured out just so those on the receiving end can say they've had an experience. He is never given so that we can become bloated with pride. In the days that followed, these people didn't have time to sit around making this outpouring of God's Spirit a shrine. Neither can we.

The answer to their prayers went beyond the outpouring of the Spirit and took directions these people never could have anticipated. They were molded into a community characterized by selfless generosity and powerful witness (Acts 4:32-37, 5:12-16). There was no hint of evil of any kind. Spiritual sensitivity and discernment were sharp, with no artificial distinctions between major and minor sin (5:1-11). The answer to their prayer included some painful twists. Their leaders were imprisoned again and beaten (5:17-42). One of their finest young leaders, Stephen, was martyred (6:8–7:60). They could recognize shifting needs, and they had the flexibility to meet them without sacrificing God-given priorities (6:1-7).

The answers to the prayers of these people included the loss of some of their homes and the fracturing of their families (8:1-4). But it also included the launching of Christianity beyond Jerusalem (8:4-40) and the conversion of the man who would become their greatest preacher, theologian, and missionary—Saul of Tarsus (9:1-31).

Would those of us who only see Christian victory in terms of our own personal success have been able to be used of God like this? It is highly unlikely, since we probably would not have prayed as they did in the first place. Theodore Roosevelt once said, "Wisdom is nine-tenths a matter of being wise in time. Most of us are too often wise after the event." So it is with victory. Most of us recognize it in retrospect. We've read the end of the story and can glibly talk about victory that we might never have recognized had we lived back then. Christian victory is defined in the terms of the kingdom of God, not in the terms of this world. It is not always immediately apparent. It may not be for years—maybe not until eternity.

Margaret was part of a new church we were attempting to launch. An elderly woman who was very active and visible in the community, she hosted Bible studies in her home, visited, and did many things to help the infant church get started. A pastor was called and things looked good.

But soon problems surfaced that would eventually kill this embryonic group. The church acquired a bad name and became a target of ridicule. No one felt this as much as Margaret. Other families moved. The pastor left. But Margaret had lived there for thirty years and it was home. So she stayed and endured the taunts and took the ridicule that the behavior of others deserved. Her reputation took a pounding.

We sat together at lunch after loading the church's remaining few possessions into a U-Haul trailer. Expecting her to be bitter, I asked, "Now what will you do since we've closed down the church?" Her eyes lit up as she asked if she could keep the bank account open. She wanted to use some of the remaining money to advertise a Bible study in her home that might still become that badly needed church. Slightly in awe and caught off guard, I agreed.

A few months later the checkbook came in the mail, along with a note saying that the Bible study hadn't materialized. She also said that if we ever wanted to start a church in her area again, she wanted to be part of it. I knew Margaret too well to mistake this for spiritual bravado, a pretense to disguise pain. She was open about her pain. Margaret was a woman who did not need visions and feelings to keep her going. She knew that victory meant doing God's will regardless of circumstances or outcome. While she never saw results like those of Peter and John, she belongs to their number—the fellowship of the unstoppable.

How people pray says a lot about how far into eternity they can see. I once heard a man say in prayer, "Lord, some of us feel the rain while others just get wet." I want not only to say this prayer but also to live it. I want to feel the rain, to have my spiritual senses alive to God's concerns on this dying planet. The Lord's Prayer is the heart song of all who seek God's kingdom. The Christians in Acts 4 cry out joyfully across centuries and from heaven to hallow His name, advance His kingdom, and accomplish His will. The urge to sing along in heart is strong. Besides, haven't we all spent too much of our frightfully short lives merely being wet, living under what a friend calls "the sodden goodies of existence"—a debilitating absorption with daily bread, security, and prudence that another man described as "that dismal fungus"?

9
Fellowship of the Unclean

———◆———

Many of my Saturday nights as a small child were spent at a nearby shopping center. It was the place to go and meet people, whether you shopped or not. One night I saw a man sitting on the sidewalk with a blanket spread out in front of him. On the blanket were pencils, small wind-up toys, and all kinds of things that any five-year-old would love.

My dad's voice caught my ear. He motioned for me to come over next to him. "Don't just stand there, David," he said. "It's not nice to look at people who are like that." Like what? I hadn't noticed that the man didn't have legs. He just seemed like a nice guy selling great stuff.

Standing there by my father's side that evening I learned something. A lot of people passed by, and the guy was impossible to miss. If you didn't see him you certainly could hear his snappy jokes and patter, which I thought were very funny. Suddenly I realized why nobody seemed to see him. They didn't want to. They were ignoring him. I stood there feeling the innocent outrage of a five-year-old against those mean people who were afraid of a man just because he didn't have any legs. Little did I know then that

I would grow up to become one of those people, with a fear that makes a person both mean and blind.

In biblical times, lepers would have to cry "unclean!" as they walked down the street so that others could avoid them. We don't meet many lepers today, but we meet others who don't need to say anything to distance us.

Ten minutes spent in any of the gospels will show that Jesus Christ paid considerable attention to people many of us avoid if we can. The lepers, the blind, the physically deformed, the morally scandalous, the demon possessed, the hated and alienated—all found to their amazement that this well-known Rabbi readily ministered to their needs with dignity and compassion. He was merely reflecting His Father's heart.

Anyone who in Christ's name sets out in pursuit of the kingdom of God will soon learn that the recipients of that kingdom have already been targeted. We are to love the people no one else will love. When you follow Christ, you forfeit the sins of loving selectively and the intentional blindness that renders people such as that legless man invisible. You walk in the footsteps of One who stands as the most amazing spectacle man can witness—the living God, who relentlessly seeks a crushed humanity that has rebelled against Him.

THE INVISIBLE POOR

We were six white college students in a black neighborhood of a southern city. Sitting in front of a row of flats was quite an education for the son of a middle-class steel worker. I'd never even seen a cockroach before. I saw thousands that night.

Working out of a mission situated between the black projects and the ramshackle hovels of the poor whites took some getting used to. We learned to live with the thick smell of fried food, cheap wine, sweat, and urine that assaulted the nose from behind every opened door.

Jesus said, "The poor you have with you always" (Matthew 26:11). They're certainly with us in America by the millions. And who can begin to count the poor throughout the world? Whether we live in city housing projects or in a middle-class suburb, poverty affects everyone.

There are many reasons why the poor are still with us. Economic policies allow outside investors to carry off the lion's share of dollars generated by the often underpaid labor of locals. High illiteracy rates make thousands, even millions, unemployable. War, revolution, and armed conflict of all kinds send refugees scurrying in droves across borders into neighboring countries that can't support their own population, let alone the throng of people coming in. Errors of ecological ignorance fuel famine for millions. The explosion of urban populations around the world in places like Mexico City ensure that someday there will be slums larger in population than Chicago—an urban glut that will imprison hundreds of millions.

Our response to all this has most often been one of avoidance. Many of us have gone to great lengths to live in areas where we and our children don't have to look at poverty unless there's something about it on the evening news. In our town there's a particular grocery store that many people absolutely avoid because mostly low-income people shop there.

Often the church chooses to distance itself from the poor. Could it be that the church has headed for the suburbs for the same reasons as everyone else? City church buildings now boarded up or converted to something else testify not to progress but to tragedy. Maybe the members tired of chasing transients and street people from their sleeping places around the church doors on Sunday morning. Or maybe they worried about their cars being vandalized. There might have been concern that the church would no longer draw the "right" kind of people if it remained downtown. But they're gone to where they can worship without being disturbed by what's outside the front door.

> It is our shame and disgrace today that so many Christians—I will be more specific: so many of the soundest and most orthodox Christians—go through this world in the spirit of the priest and the Levite in our Lord's parable, seeing human needs all around them, but (after a pious wish, and perhaps a prayer, that God might meet them) averting their eyes, and passing by on the other side. That is not the Christmas spirit. Nor is it the spirit of those Christians—alas, they are many—whose ambition in life seems limited to building a nice middle-class Christian home, and making nice middle-class friends, and bringing up their children in nice middle-class Christian ways, and who leave the sub-middle-class sections of the community, Christian and non-Christian, to get on by themselves.[1]

A friend pastors in a nearby city. His church decided to move out of the center of town and build a large church in a newly developing subdivision. The church moved but Tom stayed because he was called to the need of the neighborhood, which still remained even if the church left.

Starting from scratch, his new church struggles financially in an old building and engages every kind of need a run-down neighborhood provides. While he's pastored large churches, Tom would tell you that he's doing some of his richest ministry now.

Entrepreneurs and home owners are going back into the city. So why not start a church to serve the poor? A word of advice: Don't expect results quickly. Most church growth strategies don't work with the poor. Churches that make well-intentioned but misinformed forays into poverty areas don't last long. You may spend a lot of time ministering to people who may never join your church, serving them just because they're needy.

Yet no one is exempt from helping the poor. You may not think there is much poverty around you. But you might be surprised. While much of what I've said focuses on the urban poor, poor people are almost everywhere. In our small Midwestern town, people find breakfast in the dumpsters behind the supermarket. Broken-down cars containing large families and their belongings from time to time have rolled to our door. It's like something from John Steinbeck's *Grapes of Wrath.*

There are needy people within our churches whose needs aren't being met. Unexpected crises can add others to the ranks of the poor. But know for certain that Jesus meant what He said:

> "The King will say to those on His right, 'Come, you who are blessed of My Father, inherit the kingdom prepared for you from the foundation of the world. For I was hungry, and you gave Me something to eat; I was thirsty, and you gave Me drink; I was a stranger, and you invited Me in; naked, and you clothed Me; I was sick, and you visited Me; I was in prison, and you came to Me.'
>
> "Then the righteous will answer Him, saying, 'Lord, when did we see You hungry, and feed You, or thirsty, and give You drink? And when did we see You a stranger, and invite You in, or naked, and clothe

You? And when did we see You sick, or in prison, and come to You?'

"And the King will answer and say to them, 'Truly I say to you, to the extent that you did it to one of these brothers of Mine, even the least of them, you did it to Me.'" (Matthew 25:34-40)

People who claim to love God from the healthy side of a checkbook balance or from a home filled with all the modern conveniences and luxuries need to weigh carefully what Jesus says here.

THE EMPTY RICH

Another group we need to serve is the rich. Who wouldn't like to "minister" to rich people? Pastors and church treasurers with visions of budget deficits and building programs swirling in their heads might. That's exactly the problem. Who will love the rich simply for who they are and not for the financial difference they can make on a church, ministry, or favorite cause?

The rich are accustomed to having people "hit on them." Everybody wants something, and the church is sometimes merely standing in line along with everyone else. Church leaders learn to cut deals over lunch and golf. Walk along Chicago's Gold Coast, the domain of high-rise high rollers, or drive through Detroit's Grosse Point. Sophisticated security systems along with tall hedges and fences buy the isolation that too often provides seclusion from the onslaughts of the needy and, more likely, the greedy.

We once did a survey in our part of town on community needs. A local television station got wind of it and asked me whether there were any needs in this part of town since it was filled with many highly paid professionals. The truth is that there are constantly many needs of the heart that dollars can't fill. Many people learn the hard way the truth of Jesus' words in Luke 12:15 when He said, "Not even when one has an abundance does his life consist of his possessions." These same people know the pain of divorce, substance abuse, suicide, and every other heartache currently crushing humanity.

If God is no respecter of persons, neither is He a respecter of net worth. Jesus did not lessen the standards of His kingdom to accommodate a rich young man (Luke 18:18-25). Neither should we accommodate someone who wants to take control of a ministry with a checkbook. But Jesus also looked past the wealth of a man named Zaccheus to see a hungry heart. Christ didn't care if the man had a red cent to his name.

A man owning several businesses once asked me, "Dave, who reaches out to guys like me?" Surely it is the people of Jesus who must deny their materialistic cravings and blind themselves to the affluence modeled in our culture. Someday the rich will stand before God, who is not at all enamored with or impressed by their wealth. Whether they stand there in judgment or in grace may largely depend on how well we understand how to approach them in a godly, not mercenary, way.

THE UGLY-SOUL PEOPLE

We also need to start seeing another part of the fellowship of the unclean: the ugly. Their ugliness has relatively little to do with their appearance, but is an ugliness of spirit. These are the ones whose sin is robust and scarlet. They are often ugly in the sight of many Christians because of the harsh and condescending way we grade sin and sinners.

I was once told of a particular family's opinion of their children. They think their kids are pretty good. But "good," it seems, means that their kids don't murder and pillage (at least not in excess!). It's so easy to start grading sin. Sin that's really bad is usually always worse than what *I* do—which I will quickly point out when confronted.

God doesn't find those caught in gross trespass any harder to forgive than anyone else. All sin (even ours) is gross to God. There are certain people we avoid or who make us uncomfortable. But since God sees us all in the same predicament, we should ask for grace to drop the pretense of being better than these "ugly" people in some way and to reach out. Our pride needs the wounding, and their eternity hangs in the balance.

Who, for example, will reach out to homosexuals? All gay rights name-calling and rhetoric aside, some of us really are homophobic. We hate and fear homosexuals. Our Midwestern city had its first gay rights rally not long ago. The local paper splashed a picture across the front page of a local pastor cheek-to-jowl with one of the demonstrators. There was no mistaking the anger and hatred there.

A woman named Susan and her sister wanted to find a way to let homosexuals in our town know that while God hates all sin, He loves sinners. It worked out that a team in the city volleyball league made up completely of lesbians had two openings. So Susan and her sister joined that team as a witness to those women. It wasn't easy. Plenty of people knew about the team and turned out to shout insults and all manner of foul remarks. They assumed that Susan and her sister were lesbians, too, and so the sisters took a share of the abuse.

Something deep inside most of us would have screamed to let that crowd know that we were in no way like these others. But these two women kept their mouths shut and willingly took the jeers along with the rest of the team. The other team members noticed this special sense of sacrifice, and they began to ask questions. They were dumbfounded as to why two women would take undeserved abuse and honestly care for them when others showed only hate.

The whole issue of sexual sin is another area where we need to embrace the fellowship of the unclean. Be it adultery, sexual abuse of children, pornography addictions, or any other sexual problem, we need to face these things squarely instead of ignoring them because of shock or repulsion.

Since the Bible discusses the common nature of sin so clearly and in such great detail, we should realize that anyone is capable of just about anything. All of the world's sexual sin can be found in the church. In many congregations, some of the soundest Christians we know may carry terrible secrets.

A number of years ago I directed the visiting program of our church. One night I mistakenly sent two women to see a young man who had previously attended regularly. When they arrived, he seemed awkward and uncomfortable. The ladies could see over his shoulder to the living room where a movie projector had been set up. Pictures were spread out everywhere. The man clearly had a pornography addiction. We never saw him again. Now that his secret was exposed, he moved. No one would have guessed the problem in this particular man.

I asked the director of the local information and referral service about which problematic segments of society did not have support groups. She said, "That's easy. It's sexual abusers. Nobody wants to have anything to do with them." Jesus knew how to deal with those in sexual sin—firmly yet compassionately (John 4:7-26, 8:3-11). The sexual freedom so loudly trumpeted during the last twenty years or so is a hideous bondage enslaving many. The true liberation in Christ of people addicted to immoral sex will be accomplished only by those who can see past the sin to just another fellow sinner. Sexual abusers already have enough condemnation of their own without us piling our disgust and condemnation on top of it.

The divorced are also full-fledged members of the fellowship of the unclean. Their number is increasing at an alarming rate. While their lives scream with needs, including sin that needs to be forgiven, they often find the church looking the other way. But certainly their sin is not the unforgivable sin. Neither is substance abuse. And how about suicide? Can real Christians become suicidal? If our theology is primarily constructed to hide us from the reality of sin we'll say no. If we've graded sin so that Christians are only guilty of the "lesser" ones as opposed to the really "big" ones, we'll say no. If our church is a nice place where nice people do only nice things, we'll be of no help to those dropping on all sides.

But people who are truly dedicated to God's kingdom find themselves loving the same kind of people Jesus loved. A lot of these are people no one else will touch. Sure, there are costs. We could be lied to, ripped off, used, taken advantage of, and possibly even sacrifice our lives. But people who seek first God's kingdom are not obsessed with self-interest, so it's no big deal to them how they're treated.

Some people think that they really don't have the opportunity to do anything. They need to be honest with themselves about their "lack" of opportunity.

Opportunities come in so far as we really want them. If we are reluctant to share our faith with others, however plausible our excuses may be, opportunities will not readily come, or else we shall not see them or take them. But if we genuinely long that others should know the love of Jesus that we have experienced, then, however nervous or inadequate we may feel, constant natural situations will present themselves, and the Spirit's love within us will overcome the obvious barriers of age, class, education, race or culture that may exist.[2]

Sometimes it may be necessary to choke down unwillingness to be involved with or even to see "ugly" people. In the eyes of God we're neither unlike nor above them.

For we also once were foolish ourselves, disobedient, deceived, enslaved to various lusts and pleasures, spending our life in malice and envy, hateful, hating one another. But when the kindness of God our Savior and His love for mankind appeared, He saved us, not on the basis of deeds which we have done in righteousness, but according to His mercy, by the washing of regeneration and renewing by the Holy Spirit. (Titus 3:3-5)

The "unclean" are multiplying rapidly as our culture is disintegrating at all levels of life, including the level of the so-called untouchables. Their ugliness to society is part of the crashing weight of consequences they cannot escape. People in this condition can be amazingly open to the voice of Christ. In every culture, the Spirit of God has cut deep into the ranks of the unclean to reap great harvests for God's kingdom. But who will go? Who will speak? Who will take this stance?

I stand by the door,
I neither go too far in, nor stay too far out,

The door is the most important door in the world—
It is the door through which men walk when they
     find God.
There's no use by going way inside, and staying there,
When so many are still outside and they, as much as I,
Crave to know where the door is.

And all that so many ever find
Is only the wall where a door ought to be.
They creep along the wall like blind men,
With outstretched, groping hands.
Feeling for a door, knowing there must be a door,
Yet they never find it . . .
So I stand by the door.

The most tremendous thing in the world
Is for men to find that door—the door to God.
The most important thing any man can do
Is to take hold of one of those blind, groping hands.
And put it on the latch—the latch that only clicks
And opens to the man's own touch.
Men die outside that door, as starving beggars die
On cold nights in cruel cities in the dead of winter—
Die for want of what is within their grasp.
They live, on the other side of it—live because they
     have not found it.
Nothing else matters compared to helping them
     find it,
And open it, and walk in, and find Him . . .
So I stand by the door.

The people too far in do not see how near these are
To leaving—preoccupied with the wonder of it all.
Somebody must watch for those who have entered

the door,
But would like to run away. So for them, too,
I stand by the door.
I admire the people who go way in.
But I wish they would not forget how it was
Before they got in. Then they would be able to help
The people who have not yet even found the door,
Or the people who want to run away again from God.
You can go in too deeply, and stay in too long,
And forget the people outside the door.
As for me, I shall take my old accustomed place,
Near enough to God to hear Him, and know He
      is there,
But not so far from men as not to hear them,
And remember they are there, too.
Where? Outside the door—
Thousands of them, millions of them.
But—more important for me—
One of them, two of them, ten of them,
Whose hands I am intended to put on the latch.
So I shall stand by the door and wait
For those who seek it.
"I had rather be a door-keeper . . ."
So I stand by the door.[3]

One day a man lingered on the front steps of our church until everyone was gone. He had attended occasionally, and we'd had some good talks at his apartment. Carl said he wanted to apologize. I couldn't imagine what he wanted to apologize for, so he explained.

His life had been hard. At one point it became so bad that suicide seemed to be the only escape. He attempted to hang himself but used an old rope, which snapped—but not until he'd hung for at least a minute or two, feeling that noose strangling his life away before he fell to the floor.

"That's why I want to apologize. You see, to this day I can't stand to wear a tie or button my collar. I can't stand anything tight around my neck. I hope you or your folks here weren't offended. Dave, does God understand why I can't wear a tie?"

My throat was tight but I managed to get it out, "Of course He understands if you don't wear a tie."

"I'm really glad," Carl said, "because I've never found God the way I can sense Him in this little church." Then he shook my hand and walked away. My eyes were full as I went into the empty church and sat down. Every once in a while the Spirit of God lets you know you're doing something that honors Him. Christ had honored us unawares by allowing us to touch Carl. All I could say was, "Lord, bring more."

Years ago as a young boy, I stood angry as people ignored a crippled man selling trinkets on a sidewalk. Now I take my kids to Chicago where, while we are riding the "El," they point to a group of people and say loud enough for everyone in the railway car to hear, "Look, Dad, there's a lady with a ruby in her nose!" After I crawl back out from under my seat I say, "Don't stare at people like that."

When the deaf man soliciting at O'Hare Airport comes by, I'm strongly tempted to look the other way. Left to myself, I've come full circle. But thanks to Christ, I'm breaking free. And as we grow spiritually, we shall discover that our spiritual well-being is ever more inescapably entwined with the "unclean"—for the finding of their salvation and the working out of our own.

10
Who Owns Whom?

———◆———

Heads turned to look as a voice grew loud in heated agitation. There in the heart of a Latin American university a Christian student was talking with a Marxist leader on campus. The Marxist made his case plain:

> The gospel is a much more powerful weapon for
> the renewal of society than is our Marxist philosophy,
> but all the same it is we who will finally beat you. . . .
> We Communists do not play with words. We are
> realists, and seeing that we are determined to
> achieve our object, we know how to obtain the means.
> Of our salaries and wages we keep only what is
> strictly necessary, and we give up our free time and
> part of our holidays. You, however, give only a little
> time and hardly any money for the spreading of
> the gospel of Christ. How can anybody believe in the
> supreme value of this gospel if you do not practice
> it, if you do not spread it, and if you sacrifice neither
> time nor money for it . . . ? We believe in our
> Communist message and we are ready to sacrifice

> everything, even our life. . . . But you people are
> afraid even to soil your hands.[1]

Note that the Marxist wasn't faulting Christ. How could anyone not be drawn to Him? Neither was he taking a potshot at the Lord's earliest followers. Those first Christians conquered and revolutionized one of the greatest empires in world history without firing a shot. But this young Marxist was highly contemptuous of the Christians and the church he could see.

It costs to seek the kingdom of God and sometimes the price is steep. Christianity is a faith of paradoxes. And no paradox stands out more boldly than that which juxtaposes grace and the Cross. That we are saved by grace through faith is absolutely true. But we are saved into life under a Cross—a personal relationship that is paradoxically free and yet costs us everything.

We are never left to deify our own opinions as to what Jesus Christ expects of every Christian. He said, "Seek first [God's] kingdom and His righteousness; and all these things shall be added to you" (Matthew 6:33). "These things" refer to the basic needs of life. From a biblical point of view, seeking means to be completely absorbed in the search for something—to put forth a persevering and strenuous effort.

Over and above both our needs and our wants, we're to reserve our most intense efforts, our highest priorities, for Christ and His kingdom. But this is a difficult challenge. This command of Christ tends to become an uncomfortable presence in our lives. Further study shows that Jesus was not misunderstood or just being rhetorical. Scripture says without apology that obedience is the only appropriate response for all who claim to know Him (Luke 6:46-49), that a complete offering of ourselves to Him is expected

(Romans 12:1), and that once people come to Christ they belong entirely to Him (1 Corinthians 6:19-20).

Like that Marxist student, many in Western society are holding the contemporary church up to the model in Acts 2:42-47 and finding it lacking. Christ's claims steer a collision course with the gods of our age. For Christians in the United States, taking His claims seriously means going against the grain of the false gods of this world.

THE GOD OF UNCONTROLLED AMBITION

The scenario is common and repeats thousands of times. Maybe we got an inside tip, saw it posted on a bulletin board, or read it in the classifieds of a trade magazine. But a new job is open somewhere, and we get curious and itchy. We fantasize about it and finally float a few résumés just to see what happens. Whether the job comes our way or not, it's the American way to want to move up in our careers.

The Bible says many things about ambition. One example is James 3:16: "For where jealousy and selfish ambition exist, there is disorder and every evil thing." When does ambition become selfish and sinful? Sometimes we assume along with our culture that anything fulfilling our personal desires is good. And sometimes we base our self-esteem and sense of identity on the rewards of our economic system. What we do, how much we make, who is noticing us professionally—how important should these factors be in our lives?

A careful peek into the murky area of expectations and motives might be surprising. We dare not make casual assumptions about these things because we're often unaware of what is driving us. In regard to ambition, we take as a given the possibility of advancement. Often work is valued simply for where it can take us financially or positionally.

Most people would never even think of turning down a promotion, no matter the cost. Why? Because then it's highly unlikely that we would ever be considered again. Should a promotion or raise come along, the immediate response is "It must be from God."

When Jesus lays hold of a person's life, that person's ambitions become turned to the seeking of Jesus' kingdom, not his own. All selfish ambition is idolatrous ego worship. God is not primarily interested in advancing our career over His kingdom. When one comes to Christ, he forfeits any hope of guaranteed career advancement. John, James, Peter, and Andrew had worked hard to build up their fishing businesses. Matthew had a profitable (although probably unethical) career. And Saul of Tarsus was a young man on the fast track up, up, up. But then they met Jesus.

Jesus is the same today. He has not changed. As the One who now owns us, He may sovereignly decide to take us from one career to another, to prompt us to leave right in the middle of a prosperous venture for no other reason than that He can more effectively glorify His name through us someplace else. The pay may not be more, and there may even be no bright future guaranteed—except in heaven.

Every local church is a visible expression of the Body of Christ. It is put together carefully by the Holy Spirit according to gifts for service. From Christ's perspective, we live where we live and do what we do because it is His will that we advance His kingdom in this place and in this way.

So when a promotion or transfer comes along, the earthly consequences of refusing it should not be of primary consideration to those seeking the kingdom of God. There may be plenty of churches to attend in Minneapolis where I've been offered the new branch office. That's beside the point. Has Christ finished using me where I am? Does the Spirit of God want to transplant me into another part of the Body of Christ to serve Him there? Is this new job a greater challenge to glorify Christ? Are these issues foremost in my mind, or am I just using them as a flimsy excuse for yielding to the lust for more money and the ego-stroking that more authority would bring?

Just because the raise and/or promotion look good, does that necessarily mean they're from God? Can Satan use something respectable and desirable to lead men away from God's will? Before we glibly say "That door just seemed open" and phone the movers, shouldn't we make sure it was God's hand that opened the latch? When we plunge into plans without seriously reviewing them before the throne of God, do we really know better than God where we should be? Whose agenda is really first?

Christians need to answer questions like these frankly. The carnal ambition of many people has slipped the leash. The consequences hurt many. Families suffer. Children certainly suffer from frequent, poorly timed moves, as well as from absentee parents. One writes of it this way:

> Once when I was discussing a relocation with my father, he wanted to know why my generation is never satisfied. Why are we so willing to move from one state to another, to uproot our families, to disrupt friendships, all for the sake of a promotion, a new challenge, a bigger paycheck? In our rush to turn expectations into reality, have we lost sight of more important considerations?[2]

Churches suffer too. Ministry falls into disrepair or oblivion when gifted and called Christians leave before Christ wills it. Sometimes unleashed ambition invades the church. I remember an interesting conversation I had with a pastor about this subject. He told of another pastor who had completed a large building program. The church didn't really need the building. Indeed, they assumed a crippling debt in the process. "But," my friend went on, "he knew that's what you need to do in that part of the country to get the attention of a bigger church. He did, and moved on."

We need to be tough with ourselves because, as Christians, we can hide our sinful motives and ambitions under a thick blanket of spiritual-sounding jargon, deceiving not only others but ourselves. I know; I was one of the best.

After graduating from seminary I went into what became a frustrating ministry and left after a year. I said I was being called back to school for another degree, to prepare for a teaching ministry in a seminary or graduate school. Finally I decided on a graduate school in Chicago. So we loaded up our infant son and our stuff and we left. As we settled in, I soon found work and was ready to begin school when Gay became pregnant again. So I had to forget about school since I was working sixteen hours a day.

At night I would read thick theology books, pore over the seminary catalog, and fantasize about the classes I was missing. I spent long nights fueled on black coffee, railing at God because my life was in a backwater going nowhere. Anyone who knew us then would've said, "Oh, yes. Dave is called to teach, and he's waiting on God to open the way."

But one night I was forced to face the truth. I was lying awake in bed with all this on my mind. (It was always there.) Suddenly I thought I felt the bed quiver. Then it did it again. I sat up and realized that it was Gay. I asked if she was sick, only to discover she was crying! When I asked what was wrong she just sobbed and said, "Oh, nothing." But I pressed until she sat up in bed, turned and looked at me in the dark, and said, "I wish you didn't have the kids and me. We're just in your way. Then you could get on with what you want to do with your life."

Instead of getting the message, I gave superficial reassurances that really changed nothing. Within a year we moved from Chicago to North Carolina, still chasing degrees. I attended school for a semester but had to drop out for lack of funds. We were living with my wife's family, and *that* was a good thing! Money for bills was scarce.

My anger against God knew no bounds. With a splitting maul in hand, I vented it on all the red oak I could get my hands on. Gay's family had no lack of wood that winter. Why was God putting us through all this? If He wanted me to do graduate study, why wasn't it happening?

One day by the woodpile, things fell into place. Although I said God wanted me to teach, I really had been asking God to bless what I predetermined I wanted to do, partially to escape a bad experience in our first church. I really wanted a doctorate for my ego. I wanted to stand in front of a class regaling them with my pearls. God would have nothing to do with it. My clever disguise for my ambition had fooled even me. And in the process, I'd hurt my family. God spoke to my heart saying, *Dave, you can finally decide to get on with what I really want you to do with your life, or you'll bury your in-laws in firewood.*

It hurts to ask whose kingdom we're really building. But it will probably hurt us and our loved ones a lot more not to ask at all.

THE GOD OF MATERIALISM

He was the kind of man most people would be glad to have join their church. Young and sincere, the man came to see Jesus. When Jesus held him to the obedience of the Mosaic Law, the young man seemed to pass with flying colors. But Christ's eye is always on the heart, and He said, "One thing you still lack; sell all that you possess, and distribute it to the poor, and you shall have treasure in heaven; and come, follow Me" (Luke 18:22). Jesus placed His finger squarely on the man's spiritual pulse. There was something in the place in his heart where only God deserved to be. He believed in and had kept the technicalities of the Law. Possibly the commandments Jesus mentioned had never been much of a problem to keep. But although the young man thought he was worshiping God, he was actually worshiping something else.

Those who set out in pursuit of the kingdom of God are going to have to come to terms with money and what it can and cannot buy. Sometimes when working with kids I have them make bubble gum sculptures. They usually start out fine, but the more they handle the gum the stickier things get. By their nature, money and the things it can buy can be rather sticky. But Jesus had more to say: "No one can serve two masters; for either he will hate the one and love the other, or he will hold to one and despise the other. You cannot serve God and mammon" (Matthew 6:24).

Mammon (material wealth or money) is a god for all ages. It certainly commands the worship of many today. It's a deceitful god at best (Matthew 13:22). Money is deceitful on two counts. It deceives us by allowing us the illusion that we would never fall into actually worshiping it. Get a group of Christians together and mention materialism. All will agree that our society is materialistic and that it's out of control. But people find great difficulty admitting to being materialistic. The guy down the block, my boss, people who drive a certain kind of car—they're materialistic, not me.

Riches also deceive us by making us think that money can genuinely satisfy.

It is ironic that the very kind of thinking which produces all our riches also renders them unable to satisfy us. Our restless desire for more and more has been a major dynamic for economic growth, but it has made the achievement of that growth largely a hollow victory. Our sense of contentment and satisfaction is not a simple result of any absolute level of what we acquire or achieve. It depends upon our frame of reference, on how what we attain compares to what we expected. If we get farther than we expected we tend to feel good. If we expected to go farther than we have then even a rather high level of success can be experienced as disappointing. In America, we keep upping the ante. Our expectations keep accommodating to what we have attained. "Enough" is always just over the horizon, and like the horizon it recedes as we approach it.[3]

Our contemporary scene bears this out. A number of end-times prophecy and conspiracy books say disturbing things about the holograms on my credit cards. I don't know if the plastic in my wallet has a direct link to some one-world financial system. But if I were planning to seduce the most affluent, materialistic society in the history of the world, that's where I would start. Consumer credit, the business that thrives on people spending all kinds of money they don't have, racks up untold billions every year.

The shopping mall is described by many as today's entertainment center because spending is our main form of recreation. While I agree, I think spending is far more than mere recreation. If that's all it was, materialism with all its attendant ills wouldn't be the form of bondage that it is.

Spending can be a lust. I serve on a board that directs a treatment center for compulsive gamblers. At one meeting a case worker said there was beginning to be a serious need for support groups dealing with compulsive spenders.

Thanks to the technological wizardry of cable television and toll-free phone lines (with operators standing by), you can plunge yourself into crippling consumer debt without leaving the privacy of your home. And thousands, maybe more, do.

I know one woman, a Christian, whose spending became so severe that she defaulted on a number of house payments. Her husband, a salesman on the road, trusted her implicitly. Because she paid the bills, she could intercept lapse notices and creditors' phone calls. The husband didn't have a clue until the bank called to say they were repossessing the house. This incident isn't exceptional. Much of our spending may go beyond the recreational to the lustful.

Spending serves as therapy for many people. We do it to feel good about ourselves. Who hasn't treated himself to a splurge of some kind as a reward or pick-me-up on a down day? There's nothing wrong with that, unless either of two things starts to surface.

First, each of us needs to stay within bounds of what he can reasonably afford. But something much more serious comes when my self-image or self-esteem attaches itself to an insatiable lust to acquire. When I can only feel good about who I am by spending, something has gone wrong. When I cope with stress by going on shopping binges, then I'm headed for trouble.

What happens to my self-worth when I am no longer able to find discretionary cash, I've begun to pirate living expenses for binges, I've run all my credit cards up to the limit, and now I am using jewelry or even my furniture as collateral to borrow shopping funds from finance companies to be repaid at exorbitant interest?

Our society has discovered a way to camouflage this kind of thing. We simply say, "I need it." If we can dress our desires and compulsions up as needs, who can deny us? One of the secular taboos of today is that there should be anyone (especially me) who doesn't get his "needs" met. It certainly sounds more respectable than saying, "My covetousness has grown into a lust to acquire that my self-pity or self-centeredness wants to indulge right now. I don't care if it satisfies me or not. I just want it."

We can also hide from our materialistic tendencies under the pretense of paying the bills. Any expenditure becomes justifiable as soon as the monthly payments become due. Then it's a bill, and even God understands if our giving to His kingdom drops or if we have to take extra hours working overtime to pay off goodies we really wanted —doesn't He? After all, we have to pay bills, right?

A third dodge we use is to claim that we're just not rich. Of course, that all depends on who we compare ourselves to. You can have an income at the poverty level in the United States and make more money than almost ninety percent of the world's population. At that level we would be considered upper class in almost seventy percent of the world's countries. Home ownership as Americans know it is unknown in almost the whole world. All this to say that the world has good reason to view most Americans as being rich. Compared to the large majority of nations and peoples, we are. Some deeply disturbing findings reveal that all the Christians worldwide are spending over ninety-seven percent of their income on themselves.[4]

GOD OWNS IT, I MANAGE IT

How do Christians who want to please God get rid of the stickiness, the neediness, and the greediness I've described? Maybe another perspective would help since nothing is more practical than a right understanding. What we call ownership is more accurately temporary exclusive usage. In the truest sense, we never own anything. Even the biggest things like houses, land, or cars are just passing through our hands for a few short years to eventually go to someone else. We need to see that much of what we have, in fact, actually owns us. Things that need to be paid for dictate that we work, many of us at jobs we dislike, in order to pay off, maintain, insure, and finally replace what wears out. Ask any home owner about time spent maintaining or making improvements. The more you own, the more there is to be concerned and worried about.

The Bible views things differently. Instead of ownership, it speaks of stewardship. The first tenet of stewardship is that we genuinely own nothing: "For we have brought nothing into the world, so we cannot take anything out of it either" (1 Timothy 6:7). It's essentially on loan from God (Luke 12:16-20).

The second and foundational tenet is that God owns everything: "The earth is the LORD's, and all it contains, the world, and those who dwell in it" (Psalm 24:1).

While God owns everything, He has given it to us to manage with His interests and concerns in mind. We have all things He's given—including material things—to enjoy but not to worship (1 Timothy 6:17). At any time He can sovereignly decide that we do not need as much as we thought we did. Or He can pour out abundance. As the ultimate owner, He has that discretion. As the steward, we may use and enjoy material wealth, but always with an eye toward everything being managed for the glory of God and His kingdom.

One thought stands preeminent in the mind of a steward of God. The One who owns all that we manage will someday expect an accounting. The certainty of that accounting is the main point of Jesus' parable of the talents in Matthew 25:14-30. Although each servant received different amounts, each was held fully responsible for what he did with what was entrusted. Paul underscored the same theme in 1 Corinthians 3:11-15.

We will give account not only as to money and possessions but also to time, opportunities, gifts, and talents. Scripture abundantly promises that all those who recognize that they're managing for His glory what only God owns will be amply rewarded. They'll also have fewer ulcers and migraines.

BREAKING FREE

How can we break free if we're caught in the web of mammon? Frankly, some of us may need to repent. These suggestions will sound strange in a materialistic age. We may have bought things that were too expensive—things that cut either into living expenses or into funds that rightfully belong to God's kingdom. Take them back if you can. If you can't, sell them and put the money against the debt. When repentance is due, equity means nothing to God. If we own things that fill up inordinate amounts of time and we cannot get these under control, then give them away. Nothing breaks the grip of materialism like giving away something you could have sold.

We may have to houseclean our attitudes. Have we cultivated appetites and material desires that will someday put us at cross-purposes with the kingdom of God? Must we always have the best that money can buy for our home and ourselves? Do labels and brand names mean more than they should?

I mentioned one day to friends that I needed new sneakers. They teased me about whether I'd buy Adidas, or maybe even a pair of Air Jordans. We laughed, and then one of them asked what size I fit. When I told her, she took the shoes off her feet—same size—and gave them to me. As she walked barefoot to the car, she assured me she had more at home. I wore them for another year until they wore out. This route may be a little extreme for some people, but our insistence on name brands on all kind of things flags some tastes that may need to be curtailed. Daily bread hardly includes Calvin Klein or Izod. We may need counseling to help identify and eradicate the root of deep compulsive patterns of consumption—counseling that helps us ground our self-esteem in Christ.

We should actively give of our money, possessions, and time to the kingdom of God. As a worthy goal or starting place, I suggest the tithe. While the New Testament does not make tithing binding upon Christians, ten percent off the top of our resources toward Christ's kingdom will go a long way toward restoring a biblical sanity to our approach to riches.

Whether we tithe or not, our giving should be systematic and generous without feeling like we're under the gun or having teeth pulled (1 Corinthians 9:7). Our giving should never be to impress anyone or even given with the idea of getting something back in return. There should be no spiritual strings attached.

Some giving should even be spontaneous. Above the tithe our family has set aside some funds as God's "mad money." Our regular giving is systematic. But this extra we've given to God to spend any way He likes, and does He ever surprise us! We could say the tithe is plenty and blow the rest on frills, but it's more exciting doing it this way. The freedom sure beats joining the ranks of Christian incarnations of Ebenezer Scrooge. Even Scrooge came to repentance from his love of money. Surely Christ's people can do so for the sake of His kingdom.

IDOLATRY AMERICAN STYLE

Between ambition and our attitude toward riches, we're really looking at something bigger that encompasses both—idolatry. Idolatry is the crowning sin of Western society. It may be our epitaph. And where does the church stand? We believe in Jesus and make all the right noises. But are we free of ambition and the love of riches? In the years ahead in the Western world, only a church that stands for Christ and His kingdom alone against the gods of the age will have credibility in the eyes of the spiritually dying.

Examining our ambitions and attitudes toward wealth is a highly personal thing. Jesus Christ does not deal with everyone in the same way. But He does deal with everyone specifically. My laying down absolutes won't help. I can't tell you how much money or possessions is enough. I can't say it's wrong to own nice things. (I own—or temporarily and exclusively use—some nice things.) Even if I could, I wouldn't, because I refuse to spare you the intrinsic struggle of allowing the Holy Spirit to probe and speak to you personally. But as one who has tried to hear a little of God's voice and has the bruises to show for it, let me suggest some areas where His voice may be heard.

What do you daydream about? Whatever has truly captured your heart, whatever you truly worship, is the stuff of your daydreams and fantasies. In idle moments, your mind will run to where your treasure is. If you are a Christian, loving the Lord with all your heart and seeking first His kingdom, there will be a God-given vision that will fuel the desire to glorify Him in some way that surfaces in your daydreams. But if you spend substantial time with your thought life focused on moving up the corporate ladder or on various material prizes, you need to pause to consider Jesus' statement that no one can't serve both the god of money and the God of heaven.

Plans and goals are important. They are the first step of implementation for our dreams. People plan carefully for their family, professional, and financial future. What plans are being made in our lives directly concerning the advancement of the kingdom of God? Are our plans for the kingdom getting the same energy as our personal aspirations?

As we grow older change becomes more difficult. Sometimes we are compelled to change, like it or not. But those areas where we willingly submit to change are telltale indicators of what our dreaming and planning has decreed to be ultimate in our lives.

How much do we know of contentment? It's something slippery for those whose ambition and material appetites aren't curbed. They're never satisfied, no matter how much they have.

In contrast, contentment is a distinguishing mark of those who seek the kingdom of God. It definitely is an acquired taste as we're weaned from the world's incentives. It has nothing to do with how our career plans are going, how much we make, or what we can buy. "Not that I speak from want; for I have learned to be content in whatever circumstances I am. I know how to get along with humble means, and I also know how to live in prosperity; in any and every circumstance I have learned the secret of being filled and going hungry, both of having abundance and suffering need" (Philippians 4:11-12).

True contentment has far more to do with knowing beyond a doubt that we are loved unconditionally in Christ and are doing His will. That's why "godliness actually is a means of great gain, when accompanied by contentment" (1 Timothy 6:6).

Those who have contentment in Christ and the pursuit

of His kingdom don't cast furtive glances over their shoulders looking for greener pastures professionally, financially, materially, or maritally. Instead, they're preoccupied with fertilizing and cultivating where He has placed them now to bear a great harvest of fruit that will glorify Him.

THE IMPORTANCE OF SACRIFICE

Sacrifice happens to be one of man's noblest impulses. There is no greater measure of what someone truly worships than noting what inspires him to sacrifice. What has knowing Christ and setting out for His kingdom cost us? It cost Paul a great deal. Yet in looking back he said, "I count all things to be loss in view of the surpassing value of knowing Christ Jesus my Lord, for whom I have suffered the loss of all things, and count them but rubbish in order that I may gain Christ" (Philippians 3:8). The King James translation uses the word *dung* in place of rubbish. That's a strong word to make an important point about sacrifice in our lives.

> When Paul says he counts the things he lost "dung," he means not merely that he does not think of them as having any value, but also that he does not live with them constantly in his mind; what normal person spends his time nostalgically dreaming of manure?[5]

We have sacrificed for job, family, house, college education, new den, summer vacation, and video cassette recorder. These things certainly aren't intrinsically evil. But again, where have we sacrificed for the kingdom of God alone, without regret or nostalgia? To think we can be followers of Christ and know nothing of this sacrifice is to be the follower of a wimp and a fraud, not of the biblical Jesus. Sacrifice is often the litmus test of worship. What is the Holy Spirit saying to us here?

Let's get painfully pragmatic. This will only take five prayerful minutes. Sit down with your pocket calendar alongside your checkbook ledger. Then ask just one question. Is God pleased with how you spend your money? If the inclination of your heart is to please God, He can bring a turnaround in a very short time.

Dave and Jan Davies were a typical couple. He ran a couple of Baskin Robbins stores, and they'd just built a brick ranch-style house in the suburbs. They attended a Bible preaching church. When he first heard his pastor's plea for volunteers to go to Brazil, Dave thought, *This is stupid. Why don't we just mail these people some money, build them a church, buy them a piano or something?* But something urged him onward. And so, without Jan, Dave went to Brazil.

On the plane ride down, he overheard two men talking. One asked if anyone from Dave's church had come. The other replied that there was one fellow (referring to Dave) but that he couldn't do anything! Dave was aghast, but that's just how he felt—he'd never taught or even witnessed.

In Brazil Dave was unprepared for the poverty he saw. He was also unprepared for something else. Entering a small village, he found the people anticipating a great evangelistic meeting. When he asked who was preaching, Dave discovered that *he* was! For two weeks he preached and witnessed.

The man who returned to Kansas wasn't the same man. Just the sight of his new home stunned him compared to what he'd seen in Brazil. Dave promptly told Jan that they would sell it and move into something smaller if they couldn't find some way to use it for the kingdom of God. Jan remembers being quick to find a way to use it!

Then God began to work on Jan. This missions thing was not just a passing fancy for her husband. During Dave's second trip overseas, Jan did some soul searching with her Bible. She sat cross-legged on the living room floor and thought of herself as a starving little girl with matted hair and ragged clothes. God said to her, "Jan, this is how you are spiritually. You're starving. You're fat materially, but you're starving spiritually." God went on to gently show her that she was a spiritual adulteress running after all kinds of "things" instead of Him. Later on she went to Bombay, India, where Christ broke her heart.

How did things change in their lives? Money that would have bought a satellite dish paid for plane tickets so that others could go overseas. Dave liked late model high-powered cars, but now he drives only secondhand cars so that the extra money can go to missions. What was to have been a luxurious family room became a suite where strangers stay for free. Foreign exchange students have used it. The Davies are opening it to a Brazilian student Dave met on his visit. She will attend college there in Topeka. Dave worked long and hard to obtain her visa. Within nine months they housed eleven foster children, abused and neglected, referred from an emergency care program.[6]

All who seek first the kingdom of God must pay the price of becoming disengaged from their driving ambition and materialism. Jesus Christ is not an advocate of the American dream. Actually He is often its enemy.

In England many years ago, a man with not much more than a grade school education went to prestigious Cambridge University to preach. While many students came with the explicit purpose of ridiculing him, he soon caught their attention. Many of them came to Christ that evening, including seven of the most brilliant, well-known students at the university.

These seven, all from wealthy backgrounds, had the potential to excel in any secular profession. But Christ and His kingdom had seized their hearts. They left everything behind that night as they responded to D.L. Moody's invitation.

These men became known as the Cambridge Seven. They all went to China where they wrote a great chapter in the history of God's kingdom. In their day, they were universally hailed as heroes. Today, I am not sure the church would respond in the same way.

When God claims our young people we say we're glad. But our conversation afterward often says otherwise. "He could have been such a good doctor or businessman." "She won't make much money doing that." Our talk betrays our hearts. A rich young ruler once came to Jesus and went away sorrowing. Those of us who have tasted of His goodness cannot let the same happen to us. We must break free from the bondage of all false gods to gain our true freedom in the kingdom of the King.

11
Dealing with Struggles

Every single human being is constantly under construction. This is certainly true in God's kingdom. There will always be at least one part of a Christian's life where the Spirit of God has torn things up so that they can be rebuilt in the image of Christ. God calls for more than just an encounter with the rough edges of life. He wants us to have an active willingness to engage in inner struggle and turmoil as a *discipline* that will fit us more for usefulness in God's kingdom. It's simply part of the cost.

We in the Western world live in an age of affluence. Our society tells us that security and comfort are of utmost importance.

> Modern Christians believe that *any* discomfort, *any* struggle, *any* period of doubt or waiting need not be. Real Christians (it is thought but never said) should never have to experience anything negative. We have given new meaning to the word "soft." We are more than soft. We are incapable of perseverance, of patience and of long-suffering.[1]

Perhaps you do not fit into this category of spoiled Christians, but no doubt you have observed this tendency of aversion to suffering and struggle, even within the church.

STRUGGLE IS JUST PART OF IT

Struggle is an essential part of the spiritual life. A profession of faith and performance in service just aren't enough. Consider the disturbing words of Jesus in Matthew 7:21-23:

> "Not everyone who says to Me, 'Lord, Lord,' will enter the kingdom of heaven; but he who does the will of My Father who is in heaven. Many will say to Me on that day, 'Lord, Lord, did we not prophesy in Your name, and in Your name cast out demons, and in Your name perform many miracles?' And then I will declare to them, 'I never knew you; depart from Me, you who practice lawlessness.'"

It is not enough to superficially say we believe in Christ and then go on our merry way. It is not enough to mechanically function in one or more church jobs. Spiritual experiences aren't enough. Jesus said that even those casting out demons and performing miracles could be self-deceived. Since not many can lay claim to such feats, His words should make us pause.

Faith itself is not easy. Those who think it is have never exercised the real thing. Faith does not mean a carefree absence of doubt, but it means acting on God's trustworthiness in spite of the doubts we have. Do we think it was easy for Abraham to go out from Ur not knowing where he was going (Hebrews 11:8) or to offer his son Isaac as God commanded (Genesis 22:1-19)? If faith is easy, then some of Jesus' sayings concerning His kingdom become quite difficult to understand: "From the days of John the Baptist until now the kingdom of heaven suffers violence, and violent men take it by force" (Matthew 11:12).

Entering God's kingdom by violence or force? C.S. Lewis said he was dragged into the kingdom kicking and screaming. Many have become Christians only after the intellectual equivalent of storming the Bastille—leveling the fortresses of ideologies and thought that are much harder to pull down than mortar and brick.

In the services at our church, we give evangelistic invitations. To Christians who have never done it, let me say that coming down an aisle is a traumatic experience. Big, strong men come shaking and with tears. Some have told me they felt the whole world was fastened on their coattails like an anchor. But still they come to exercise faith, to take hold of Christ, to strain against the gravitational pull of their own deadness with a force that Scripture calls violence.

Christian growth almost invariably involves struggle. Paul says in Galatians 5:24, "Now those who belong to Christ Jesus have crucified the flesh with its passions and desires." What he means is that, as Christians, we should consider our old lives to be nailed to the cross of Christ, stripping our sin of all power over us as we choose to live by faith in Christ (Romans 6:1-11).

I believe there is an additional reason Paul chose the metaphor of crucifixion to express what our attitude toward the flesh should be. Crucifixion was a slow, painful death. It was not the only method of capital punishment in those days. There were certainly quicker ones. Quite simply, the flesh dies hard. Few Christians bypass the feeling of certain conceit or cockiness over a rapid spurt of growth, only to fall in an area of their lives they thought was cleaned up. Christian growth involves struggle.

All those who set out to seek the kingdom of God must

pay the price of a disciplined life. Discipline is the mark where faith struggles against areas of the flesh that are in disrepair. The writer to the Hebrews said it well: "All discipline for the moment seems not to be joyful, but sorrowful; yet to those who have been trained by it, afterwards it yields the peaceful fruit of righteousness" (Hebrews 12:11).

We are continually under construction. Certain areas of life will provide spiritual workouts as long as we live. We can mark and engage them and grow. If we ignore them, our Christian life and pursuit of God's kingdom will flounder badly.

DIAGRAMING OUR DARK SIDE

One area we'll always have to face in this life is our sin. We need to not only overcome our sin, we need to study it. First we need to develop a strong spiritual early-warning system, highly sensitive to avoidance strategies that our sin employs to avoid detection. One of those strategies is *denial*. Denial says, "Who me? I don't have a problem." How many people have been destroyed by a problem they didn't have!

A second avoidance strategy is *rationalization*. It says, "I know it might look like a problem to some people but I know all the reasons why it isn't." Rationalization is world-class excuse making; it's sin with protective coloration.

Finally, there's *scapegoating*. It says, "I don't have a problem. It's *you* that's the problem—or somebody else." Scapegoating is a skunk diverting attention from itself by saying somebody else smells worse. All of these are indicators of a refusal to accept responsibility for our actions before men and God. They're ballast to be jettisoned quickly if we desire to please Christ and seek His kingdom.

Engaging in spiritual discipline means taking a closer look at temptation. Simply knowing a few things should make our defenses much stronger. The first thing to look at is *the type of temptation.* Some people are tempted by one thing; some by another. We are foolish to assume that certain things will never tempt us. It is wise to never say never.

Certain temptations have felled us many times in the past and we would do well to mark them. As the foremost tempter, Satan is a pragmatist. He will use what has worked in the past as long as it still works. His attacks in these things so well known to us should not catch us off guard.

A second dimension to note is *the timing of temptations.* Do we know when we're vulnerable? Be aware of how you react when you're fatigued—especially when you're experiencing mental fatigue. Think for a minute how you feel and respond to discouragement. The aftermath in the wake of success or an achievement is another tender spot where many have been undone.

Remember that when Satan tempted Jesus in the wilderness, he didn't come to seduce Christ immediately after He'd had the Holy Spirit descend upon Him like a dove. Satan waited until Jesus had spent forty days exposed to the elements and without food. Our enemy will strike when we are most vulnerable.

A third aspect to consider is *the degree or strength of temptations.* A simple law of biology can be applied to the area of temptations as well: If we feed something, it will grow. Hence, resolve to deal with your temptations while they are small. If you indulge, entertain, and feed them, you may not like what comes back the next time you encounter them.

HEARING GOD'S "NO"

It's not by coincidence that one of the first words toddlers learn is "no." After the first glow of coming to Christ is gone and on through spiritual middle age, an important discipline rising out of prayer involves the acceptance of God's "no." We often think others know what they're doing only in as much as they agree with us. It's hard to wean ourselves from that conception.

General Stonewall Jackson sent an order to one of his officers, in the afternoon at Malvern Hill, to advance across the open space in front of the Federal works and attack them. The officer in question hurried to Jackson, and said almost rudely: "Did you order me to advance over that field, sir?"

Jackson's eye flashed under the rim of his cap, and, in his briefest tones, he said: "Yes."

"Impossible, sir!" exclaimed the officer. "My men will be annihilated! Nothing can live there! They will be *annihilated!*"

Jackson listened in silence, but his face grew cold and rigid with displeasure. He gazed steadily for a moment at the speaker, raised his finger, and in low brief tones said: "General, I always endeavor to take care of my wounded and to bury my dead. You have heard my order—obey it!"[2]

The classroom we find ourselves in when God says "no" is where we learn about God's sovereignty. The sovereignty of God is no excuse for fatalistic, paralyzing hand wringing. Acknowledging His sovereignty means we admit that God knows what He's doing—whether or not we understand or approve. Knowing that God is in control when things fall apart or are incomprehensible is a powerful spur to keep on, to persevere. Most people learn the hard way that God's "no" means exactly that. He knows what He's doing. When He turns down our wants, He cannot be induced to change His mind the way a whiny child erodes the resolve of a weary parent.

When God says "no," instead of pouting over not getting our way we can take heart on at least two counts. First, God may be protecting us. Some of the things our children want we know as parents to be harmful or at least not in their best interests. Hindsight should remind us of many times when we can be glad God refused our request. But God also refuses our requests to teach us things that otherwise we might never learn—things more important than getting our way.

When I was twelve, I bought an album by Count Basie's band that changed my life. I was just a fledgling musician, but I suddenly fell in love with jazz. Moreover, I decided that I wanted to play it. I began to learn on an instrument rented from the school, but a couple of years later I wanted my own. I went to ask my dad for the money for a bass fiddle. He must have seen this coming. He said that it was out of the question; it was just too expensive. However, he did say I could get a job and earn the money myself. So, I found a job cleaning a jewelry store—and I learned about the value of a dollar and the satisfaction of hard work toward a goal. These were things I wouldn't have learned had my father not said "no." Instant gratification—material or spiritual—poisons the cisterns of many lives.

GOD'S LABORATORY OF LIFE

It was a winter I will always remember. First, there was that one week before Christmas. On Monday, a local funeral director asked me to perform a service for a man I'd never met. During the service my heart ached for his sobbing wife and a four-year-old daughter whose daddy would have been alive if he'd been wearing a seat belt.

On Wednesday, I got a phone call from a young seminary couple we were working with. Pregnant just two months, the wife had had a miscarriage. I went and sat with them in their apartment, praying and crying together.

On Friday, George, our kids' chameleon, died. While a chameleon's death does not compare in magnitude with the untimely death of a young father or with a miscarriage, my children's grief was quite real. My young son, Steve, trying to be a man for his younger sister, had dug a hole into the dirt frozen under new snow. My little girl, Karen, and my wife brought George in a small box. He'd been lovingly wrapped in tissue and the box also had a farewell note inside that we'd all signed. I read Scripture and prayed (parents and pet owners will understand).

Karen tenderly placed the box in the hole, which Steve gently filled in. From somewhere they produced a red silk carnation that they placed on the snow. Karen buried her face in her mother's coat. Steve's chin trembled. As I looked on, something wet began to freeze on my cheek.

On Christmas Day, my wife's grandfather died. He was always quick with a pearl of truth, a laugh, or a hug. In my memory we still chug lazily down through his corn field on the tractor, where he let me drive while he rode on the hitch and told me about life. When the wind was right, I caught the scent of honest sweat and the sweet smell of juice from Black Mariah chewing tobacco. When he died, his wife, who had Alzheimer's disease, not only didn't grieve but didn't remember she had a husband.

Three weeks later I drove across three states to be with my mother, who was undergoing surgery for cancer. As an afterthought, while driving back from the hospital, I pulled into the cemetery and visited my dad's grave for the first time, even though he'd been dead for thirteen years. That night before I went back into the hospital, I sat on the bumper of my car and watched the snow begin to fall through the amber lights of the parking lot. I looked up, closed my eyes, drew in a deep breath of winter, and let it out slowly. It had been quite a month and a half.

How deeply the lives of human beings can become intertwined. We are welded together across generations, decades, and miles. Almost everyone fits into a surprisingly extensive matrix of relationships. It is these relationships that God will often use as a laboratory to teach us about ourselves. Anyone seeking Christ's kingdom will find relationships changed and often costly. In view of how much our close relationships mean to us and how they affect us, the words of Christ come with the subtlety of a sledgehammer going through a plate glass window: "If anyone comes to Me, and does not hate his own father and mother and wife and children and brothers and sisters, yes, and even his own life, he cannot be My disciple" (Luke 14:26).

Christ certainly isn't advocating active hatred of anyone, let alone those most dear to us. But He does mean that our relationship with Him is to have preeminence over the claim of any, even the closest, human relationship. Our love for Him is to be of such magnitude that the strongest love possible between humans resembles hate by comparison.

Perhaps the most costly discipline many Christians will be compelled to tackle is in the area of relationships. Jesus Himself paid this price. He sometimes endured strained relationships with both His family and the hometown people who'd known Him all His earthly life (Matthew 13:54-57).

Coming to Christ and beginning the pursuit of His kingdom will bring tension and confusion into some of our relationships almost overnight. I remember phoning home from college and telling my dad about all Christ was doing in my life. There was a lot of silence on his end. Finally one night he said, "David, if you're part of some strange group, I'm going to yank you off that campus so fast it'll make your head spin." He later took a closer look, and everything was fine. But it doesn't always end that way. Jesus warned that this might happen:

> "Do not think that I came to bring peace on the earth; I did not come to bring peace, but a sword. For I came to set a man against his father, and a daughter against her mother, and a daughter-in-law against her mother-in-law; and a man's enemies will be the members of his household. He who loves father or mother more than Me is not worthy of Me; and he who loves son or daughter more than Me is not worthy of Me." (Matthew 10:34-37)

Sometimes, through no fault of our own but purely due to our stand for Christ, those closest to us will become alienated. Two friends of mine, one from India and the other of Jewish descent, were disowned by their families when they learned they'd become Christians. Another friend, a Pakistani, told me of the trials of his father becoming a Christian. His grandfather made at least two attempts on the life of his own son, once by poison and another by loosing a pack of dogs after him. ("They were big dogs, David, the kind that take your flesh away," he said.)

Another friend went home from college one weekend excited to tell her family of her new faith in Christ. When I saw her the following Monday, I noticed that the left side of her face had a huge bruise. But apparently while her father didn't understand, he came to discover that her faith in Christ could not be beaten out of her.

One of the most difficult relationships where Christ must be preeminent is marriage. It's impossible to overestimate the extent of influence one mate has over another. In marriage every area of our life is affected to the core by our spouse. That's why the Bible is clear and to the point: "Do not be bound together with unbelievers; for what partnership have righteousness and lawlessness, or what fellowship has light with darkness?" (2 Corinthians 6:14).

In other words, if God wills that we marry, we are never free to marry someone who is not a Christian. By Christian, Paul did not mean someone who believes in God or who goes to church once in a while. In context, he surely meant someone who has experienced spiritual regeneration through the Holy Spirit by trusting completely in the atoning death of Jesus Christ for the forgiveness of his sins. We are only allowed to marry someone else like us, who loves Jesus Christ with all his heart, soul, and mind. Christ owns us and is not about to bless our union with someone with whom He would have to compete for the rest of our lives.

Many people who were about to marry an unbeliever have told me they didn't think that their unbelieving mate would change their beliefs. I respond by saying that their beliefs aren't the issue; their obedience is. Entering into such a marriage would be a step of disobedience. And what would the rest of the marriage be?

I occasionally get to share this message with college students. It's much like smearing one's hand with bacon grease and then thrusting it into a tank of piranhas. After one such encounter a girl came up to me and asked to talk. She had had a couple of bad experiences with guys, but now she was seeing a guy who treated her well. She was a Christian and he was not. I could tell that much of her self-esteem relied on this guy and that she was afraid to make an issue of her faith because she might lose him.

My heart went out to her because I knew how she felt. I gave up a relationship in college because the girl wouldn't commit herself to Christ. Today I could go back and show you where I sat on the curb and watched her walk out of my life. It was hard then, and it hurt. But three years later God honored it. He never honors disobedience. In over twenty years of being a Christian, I've never seen one person lead a vibrant Christian life who voluntarily, knowingly married a nonChristian. All have known heartache and compromise, and some have encountered shipwreck.

Other relationships in your life may come under construction as well. Rebellious adolescents and preoccupied college students may need to learn about honoring parents. Parents may need to stop ignoring and squelching their children. Husbands may need to learn to love their wives as Christ loves the church. Wives may need to learn to submit to their husbands as unto the Lord. (I only mention this to be fair both ways. Actually most Christian wives I've met don't have trouble so much with biblical submission. The problem can be that the man to whom they must submit isn't much like Christ and isn't trying very hard to change.)

The snags in relationships may show us how unloving we truly are, or how full of ourselves we can be. But in any event, they will bring us to a greater dependence on Christ to flesh Himself out in all our rough places. And He will.

DEALING WITH QUIRKS

At camp one summer, Bill came to me and asked me to pray for him to stop biting his nails. Some people might consider his request humorous or maybe trivial. Nail biting doesn't exactly compete with armed robbery, and it is hardly the unforgivable sin. All of us have habits. Many are nothing more than idiosyncrasies that help express our personalities. For example, I will eat all of one thing on my plate before eating anything else.

Our habits may seem innocent enough, but sometimes the Spirit of God will flag one to be broken. Paul said in Ephesians 5:18, "Do not get drunk with wine, for that is dissipation, but be filled with the Spirit." Not only are Christians not to be under the control of alcohol, they are not to be under the control of *anything* besides the Holy Spirit.

The powerful preacher Martyn Lloyd-Jones used to smoke both cigarettes and a pipe.[3] Coming home one night, he collapsed in a chair and reached for a cigarette, only to find there were none. He began to look through the house, becoming nervous and tense. An hour passed while he ransacked the house. Finally he found half of an old mangled butt in an old pouch. He was ashamed of himself on account of his behavior.

Later Lloyd-Jones was working on a sermon when the conviction struck, "You are not free." He had never preached against smoking, and he never evidenced that he thought it sinful. But he thought his dependence on smoking was unworthy of a Christian. Nicotine had more control over him than it should, making him act sinfully toward his wife. So he quit.

Christ flags these habits to give us low-level training exercises in overcoming parts of our sinful nature by His power. The habit may be insignificant, but the exercise is not. Olympic power weight lifters don't start their careers with five hundred pound barbells. They begin years before with much lighter weights.

Don't ignore the Spirit's voice if He singles out some quirk or habit you think hardly worth noticing when He tells you that you, too, are not free. Take it as conditioning. If you follow Christ over a span of years, the bigger tests will come. If you are faithful in these lesser things, you'll have no regrets when life slaps the heavy weights on the bars.

Besides, some habits may not be as trivial as we think.

Take Bill's biting his nails. Before he asked me about pray-ing for him, Bill told me he felt called to the pastoral ministry. As such, he knew that he would spend much time in hospitals trying to comfort fearful people in all kinds of situations. How much comfort would you feel if you were waiting for the results of life-threatening surgery on a loved one and your pastor was sitting beside you gnawing his nails to the quick?

Our innocent habits can mutate into things that with the passing of years will hurt us or hinder our effectiveness for Christ. Since Jesus can see those implications where we can't, He leads us to confront them now while they're small and more easily dealt with.

IT IS A SINFUL THING TO WASTE A MIND

It is not by sheer cosmic chance that we have a brain. God gave each of us a mind and intends for us to use it. One area where we should almost always be under construction is in the discipline of thinking. In any age, it has been the ones who mastered the muscles of their mind that ulti-mately controlled the direction of their age and often the decades following. We've always needed sharp biblical thinking in our leaders. But now more than ever before, it seems that all Christians need to be as mentally strong as we can be.

In our information age where thoughts and ideas bombard us daily, we need to be able to discern the differ-ent world views that subliminally ply for admittance to our minds. The average Christian's beliefs are often not much more than a theological mulligan stew of Scripture, unex-amined opinion, tradition, and sentimental remembrance. Were we to take a test on our knowledge of Bible content, the results might surprise and embarrass us. So might a tape recording of many adult Bible classes and studies.

When one cult or another comes to the door, one of the reasons why so many people feel defensive has nothing to do with their being pushy. Actually we are intimidated by the confident ease they seemingly have with Scripture. Even if we know they're misquoting it and wrenching it out of context, we're not sure how to answer. The Bible is used to lend an air of respectability to many causes, and that's why we need to have our biblical wits about us. It is a time that calls for discernment, for thinking.

Loving Christ never bypasses the mind. It always includes thinking (Matthew 22:37, Mark 12:30, Luke 10:27). But the purpose of Christian thinking, while biblically clear, is not always realized. Paul tells us, "Do not be conformed to this world, but be transformed by the renewing of your mind, that you may prove what the will of God is, that which is good and acceptable and perfect" (Romans 12:2). One of the reasons why many Christians can remain immature so long, showing little growth or change, is that their worldly thought forms have never been replaced by biblical, godly ones, even after years of being in and around church.

One reason why some of the earlier spiritual awakenings penetrated to the very depths of culture was because of the intellectual force of some of the leaders. Men like Jonathan Edwards and Timothy Dwight were not only effective pulpiteers; they also served as the presidents of Princeton and Yale respectively.

Scripture is much more than a collection of proof texts; it's a tool for building a comprehensive view of all of life—a grid by which every thought, attitude, action, and ethic is measured. A church that tries to contend for the faith without thinking will be cut down quickly (Jude 3). Thinking people outside of Christ are suspicious, even insulted, when they are asked to suspend their thinking. They should be.

Christian thinking is more than having answers for the next cultist on our doorstep. We must do battle in the marketplace of ideas. We must not stop at just converting individuals. We must aim at transforming the mindset of our culture. What many of us don't know is that almost every field of human thought and endeavor in Western culture was either midwifed or strongly advanced by Christianity. It is hardly possible to point to an area where the leading individuals in its particular history either were not Christians or didn't operate on Christian presuppositions— science, medicine, law, philosophy, art, etc.

Today these areas of life and thought posture as *secular* bastions in our culture. But the only reason they can do this is that the church has intellectually surrendered the field. That is changing, but not fast enough. God is raising up scholars in every field of endeavor. But the *whole* church is called to destroy speculations and every lofty thing raised up against the knowledge of God, to take every thought captive to the obedience of Christ (2 Corinthians 10:5).

How do we start? Read the Bible. Many Christians never do. Brilliant minds writing thousands of commentaries haven't exhausted it. Learn to handle the different types of literature. The Bible is really a library of books that need to be handled well individually. Trace major themes as they wind through hundreds of years. Study helps are available. All it takes is *time*.

A dip into history, especially church history, would prove far more fascinating than you could imagine. How did we get from the book of Acts to today? Ministers and individuals ignorant of the scope of our heritage not only end up reinventing the wheel, but also sometimes puncture it the way it was originally flattened hundreds of years ago. People seeking the kingdom of God in this rapidly moving and dying age have no time to waste on mistakes made out of ignorance that have already been made long ago and should be avoided another time.

The reading of biographies is a great help and encouragement to believers. Be sure to get honest ones. Some are written by admirers who, although well-intentioned, sometimes obscure parts of a life.

Spiritual classics, those books whose titles everyone knows but few have read, should make our list. Actually *read* C.S. Lewis's *Mere Christianity* or Blaise Pascal's *Pensées*. Feeding on minds that have gripped their age can model for us how it is done. Some carefully selected secular literature should cross our path as well. A college in the next state is privileged to have a substantial part of the personal library of Charles H. Spurgeon, the insightful preacher. A brief scanning of the shelves will show that Spurgeon was familiar with the major secular works of his day in many fields. Books by Darwin and Hegel are dog-eared and scrawled with comments.

Back in my college days, one of my professors had learned of my new faith. He was somewhat of a skeptic toward Christianity. One day he lent me a copy of *The Future of an Illusion* by Sigmund Freud, asking for my opinion. The book was a mind opener. I digested Freud's ideas and interfaced them with Scripture. What light and discernment did Scripture shed on Freud's ideas? When I returned the book, I spent an hour or so witnessing to the professor while discussing the book. Learning to engage formidable ideas on their own secular turf puts teeth in our bite intellectually.

HOW TO ACT IN A CONSTRUCTION ZONE

Disciplines in any area are difficult. If they were no problem, Christ wouldn't have placed us under construction or discipline in the first place. But when the Lord points out some area of our life that needs attention, we have a way of making it tougher on ourselves than He ever intended. Here are some ways to help ourselves even when growing is difficult.

Set realistic goals. Many Christians are zealous activists for Christ. But this can hurt if we do ourselves in by expecting more than what is realistic.

I once tried to iron the kinks out of my spiritual life by revamping my quiet time. I wanted to read a devotional followed by eight chapters of Scripture. Then I wanted to memorize two verses a day and do memory review. Then I would spend time in portions of a rather extensive prayer notebook, read one chapter from a spiritual classic, and conclude with singing some hymns of praise. Oh, yes, I wanted to do all this in one hour. I was so busy watching the clock and checking things off my list that not much communion with Christ went on. I just expected too much.

Start small. If God has convicted you of a relationship that needs work, taking that person to lunch or buying a birthday gift may not be the first step. Maybe just speaking a civil and genuinely warm "good morning" without choking is a better place to start.

Don't be ambushed by failure; expect it. Quite frankly, because we're sinners, perfection will elude us until we get to heaven. Remember those realistic goals we were to set? We're going to blow them eventually, somewhere, sometime. Such failure tends to make us discouraged. We want to quit. Did you sleep in past your quiet time again? Did you break the diet and slink off to bury your sorrows by killing a box of Girl Scout cookies or a package of Hostess Ding Dongs? By not allowing for failure, you give it additional power to derail you when it comes. Remember that in discipline in any area of life, you are attempting to alter or eradicate patterns that are deep-seated. They took a long time to get there. Instilling new patterns will likewise take time, probably longer than you think. Don't fool yourself. It won't be easy.

Live by faith and not by works. Remember all the things I was trying to stuff into my spiritual life? I failed. It was inevitable. When I did fail, I was convinced that God was down on me because I couldn't perform up to my own expectations. The operative word is *perform*.

Thousands, who theologically believe in salvation by grace through faith live believing in their everyday lives that God loves them only when they perform well. Christianity runs on grace. Every other religion and sect in the world runs on performance. Jesus Christ gives forgiveness and fresh starts thousands of times over for everyone who follows Him. Determine now not to be crushed by failure. It will surely come. Jesus will not be surprised when it does. His grace will be waiting, ready to forgive, cleanse, and rearm your resolve to go again—thousands of times.

How can I tell if I'm making it? It's the natural thing to want results, but Christ sometimes calls us into the discipline of being under construction in areas where it's difficult to see if we're making any progress. Sometimes there are visible rewards when new behavior patterns and habits have been ingrained by the power of Christ. Those times are their own reward. The sheer rightness of the attempt is another mark of being on the right track. When we know that our motives are to glorify and please Christ, especially in something the world fully approves, the sheer desire to make the attempt to change is evidence of the presence of Christ's Spirit.

People bereft of God's Spirit feel no need for such changes or renovations. In these cases, even if we are completely mistaken about Christ touching a particular area, He is certain to correct our course to where He really wants to work as long as our motives are right and the willingness to accept and attempt the discipline are there.

Help can come from unexpected directions. A reporter interviewing Itzhak Perlman, the accomplished violinist, asked him how many concerts he played in a year. The answer was "a little over two hundred." The interviewer went on to ask how many of those were performed at Perlman's best. The great violinist thought for a second and said maybe two or three, four at most.

His answer caught the reporter by surprise. If he performed at his peak only a handful of times out of over two hundred, how was Perlman supposed to know if he was improving? With a slight grin Itzhak Perlman said, "My worst now is better than it was ten years ago."

We may be under construction in some areas all of our lives. It's natural to assume that if we cannot see results, there are none. Maybe we are looking at the wrong end of things. Crying over the results not achieved, we've not noticed that over time Christ has lifted imperceptibly the entire plane of our lives so that our worst, our failures, may be better than they were a few years ago.

Being under construction as Christ Himself deems necessary is part of the cost of seeking first the kingdom of God. Michelangelo, the noted sculptor, was seen dragging a ponderous chunk of marble down the street. When asked why he bothered, the sculptor replied, "Because there is an angel trapped in here waiting to be let out." Christ's end is neither obscure nor in doubt. Like anyone else He constructs with something in mind.

> . . . until we all attain to the unity of the faith, and of the knowledge of the Son of God, to a mature man, to the measure of the stature which belongs to the ful-

ness of Christ. As a result, we are no longer to be
children, tossed here and there by waves, and carried
about by every wind of doctrine, by the trickery of
men, by craftiness in deceitful scheming; but speaking
the truth in love, we are to grow up in all aspects into
Him, who is the head, even Christ, from whom the
whole body, being fitted and held together by that
which every joint supplies, according to the proper
working of each individual part, causes the growth of
the body for the building up of itself in love.
(Ephesians 4:13-16)

Christ calls us through the hardship of *discipline* to
bring out something only He sees in our frail weakness—
His image and likeness rising through the clay of our lives.
Like a sculptor, He will chisel away until what only He could
see is evident to all. The marble angel would win passing
praises and possibly a place in history as a museum piece.
All those submitting to Christ's chisel will have a place in
eternity. And angels looking from us to His throne will note
the resemblance with great admiration of His skill.

12
The Future of the Kingdom

Within the course of five days in early December of 1941, armed forces of Japan struck at every major American and British stronghold in the Pacific. Americans in the Philippines held out longer than most, but finally defeat seemed imminent. The last organized United States forces were on a tiny island just off Manila. One night a lone PT boat sped away from the island into the open sea to rendezvous with a submarine. A single man, General Douglas MacArthur, was considered too valuable to fall into enemy hands and was being evacuated to Australia. With the enemy on all sides and surrender near, MacArthur made what under the circumstances seemed an incredible statement. He said, "I shall return."

A PROMISE HE WILL KEEP

Speaking within the shadow of His death on the cross, Jesus Christ said some unusual things. The disciples' lives were about to be plunged into seemingly bottomless despair. It seemed like the end. However, as the powers of darkness gathered for their final assault, Christ confidently spoke of His return.

The Lord Jesus had told His men of His death to prepare them. His rallying cry was quite different. Jesus let them know they were living on a planet targeted for invasion. But He said, "I am coming back" (see Matthew 24:42-44; John 14:3,18).

After Jesus' resurrection and before the Holy Spirit was bestowed on the church at Pentecost, the disciples who watched the Lord ascend into heaven had those words reinforced by the words of angels: "Men of Galilee, why do you stand looking into the sky? This Jesus, who has been taken up from you into heaven, will come in just the same way as you have watched Him go into heaven" (Acts 1:11).

Although the kingdom of God is advancing and being built up daily, it will never rule over the nations completely until Jesus Christ returns. Those first Christians thought it might happen in their lifetime because of certain Scriptures—"The coming of the Lord is at hand" (James 5:8); "The time is near" (Revelation 1:3); "I am coming quickly" (Revelation 3:11). But as years stretched into decades and then into centuries, Christians began to realize that, while expecting the Lord is a sign of spiritual vitality, God isn't bound by man's sense of time (2 Peter 3:8-9). "Soon" has covered almost twenty centuries of human existence. Maybe one of the reasons Christ still hasn't returned is that, like Elijah watching the priests of Baal exhaust themselves in the face of a god who couldn't answer, He is waiting for all the competition and pretenders to His throne to fall by the wayside.

Some of these already have. Churchmen and theologians in the early twentieth century spoke confidently, even with a hint of swagger in their voice, that they would bring in Christ's kingdom. Two world wars crushed their

confidence into mush and in retrospect make their pro-
nouncements seem incredibly naive in the face of such a
deep and strong evil.

Religious people with good intentions cannot bring in
Christ's kingdom in their own strength and wisdom. Secular
gods have all failed to produce an antidote for the sin and
deterioration of our planet. Science, only equipped to
answer the "hows" and not the "whys," hasn't done it.
Science's handmaid technology—with Teflon, Ziploc bags,
and Nintendo—hasn't saved us either. Education hasn't
enabled us to solve immense world problems, and sometimes even to find a job. Our education has often only made
us pompous and proud of what we know instead of being
humble over what we don't. Medicine has enabled us to live
longer in the midst of a society that in too many ways values
only its young. We're living longer, but we aren't sure why.

While the secular and metaphysical gods continue to
wheeze out promises they cannot keep, Christ must be
keenly watching from beyond time and space. He alone will
return to finish the work started and carried out by His
church all these years. He will establish His kingdom.

> Then comes the end, when He delivers up the king-
> dom to the God and Father, when He has abolished
> all rule and all authority and power. For He must
> reign until He has put all His enemies under His feet.
> The last enemy that will be abolished is death. For He
> has put all things in subjection under His feet. But
> when He says, "All things are put in subjection," it is
> evident that He is excepted who put all things in sub-
> jection to Him. And when all things are subjected to
> Him, then the Son Himself also will be subjected to
> the One who subjected all things to Him, that God
> may be all in all. (1 Corinthians 15:24-28)

LIFE IN BETWEEN HIS COMINGS

As we look out into our personal future, a measly handful of decades that may or may not see Christ's return, how should we conduct ourselves? Jesus left no doubts as to how we should live. He said, "The kingdom of heaven will be comparable to ten virgins, who took their lamps, and went out to meet the bridegroom" (Matthew 25:1). This parable goes on to say how five of the virgins were wise enough to bring extra oil, while five were not and were caught unawares (25:1-13). Jesus urges all who seek His kingdom to live a lifestyle of preparedness.

One component of being prepared is to *live in a way that is vigilantly looking for His coming.* Those early Christians who expected Christ to come were not wrong to do so. Expecting the imminent return of Jesus Christ is a mark of spiritual health, even when He doesn't yet return. It's healthy because it shows two desires that are quite normal in a vibrant life.

One is the idea of heaven being our home. Home is important. It's more than just a place; it's where I genuinely belong. The concept of home strongly defines my life. Once we taste the richness of knowing Christ, the world is spoiled for us. Intuitively we know we belong somewhere else. That's why we will feel weary from time to time with the sin and evil around us, feeling out of place as if we didn't belong. The reason is that we don't. We belong in His kingdom. We will wake up in heaven and find that it's home.

Our second homing desire is simply to see Jesus. We are not only going home but home to One we love. In fact we're invited to a wedding. Invited? I should think so! We're the bride!

Anytime our hopes for the future of the kingdom of God ring with desires like this, it's a good sign. But too many people stop here. They fail to realize that being prepared involves so much more. It's not enough to want Christ to return if our desire keeps us from doing His will. The Christians in the city of Thessalonica had this problem. Some, believing the Lord was returning soon, sold all their possessions and left their jobs to wait on a hillside. Paul pointed out that expecting the Lord's return was no excuse for irresponsibility and laziness. Neither is it today.

A second component of a prepared lifestyle is *faithfulness*. Jesus said as much: "Who then is the faithful and sensible slave whom his master put in charge of his household to give them their food at the proper time? Blessed is that slave whom his master finds so doing when he comes" (Matthew 24:45-46). His return will be rather anticlimactic for anyone claiming to watch for His coming yet failing to do what Christ said to do while we wait.

Leading off another parable, Christ underscored this element of faithfulness in action:

> And while they were listening to these things, He went on to tell a parable, because He was near Jerusalem, and they supposed that the kingdom of God was going to appear immediately. He said therefore, "A certain nobleman went to a distant country to receive a kingdom for himself, and then return. And he called ten of his slaves, and gave them ten minas, and said to them, 'Do business with this until I come back.'" (Luke 19:11-13)

Doing business means taking care of the tasks assigned us—the everyday business of being a Christian. It means to keep on being the light of the world and leaven of the kingdom. What has Christ called each of us to do and to be in every area of our life? This is what we should be doing until He comes, or until we die and go to be with Him.

A third component of being prepared is *maintaining an edge for growth.* This means more than maintaining spiritual disciplines and meditating on the meaning of the kingdom of God (although it surely includes these things). Maintaining an edge for growth particularly extends to our attitudes. Jesus brought it into focus when He said, "Permit the children to come to Me; do not hinder them; for the kingdom of God belongs to such as these. Truly I say to you, whoever does not receive the kingdom of God like a child shall not enter it at all" (Mark 10:14-15).

As I write, a bunch of children are playing outside my window. They are so simple and direct.

> The first and most obvious quality about children is that they are simple—not in any derogatory sense— but children are basically uncomplicated, elemental. They go right to the heart of things. This is why children can ask such frank questions. If you pick up a little child in your arms, he is liable to look at you and say, "How come you have such a big nose?" All your adult friends have managed to evade that subject for years, but a child will come right out and ask it. They go right to the point. There is no beating around the bush, nor any pretension about them; they are forthright.[1]

A mother dragged her little girl down the street. Seeing some mica sparkle in a stone the little girl called out, "Oh, Mother, look! There are stars in the stone!" Her mother grabbed her arm and said, "Oh, come on, we haven't time for that."[2] A precious sense of wonder and mystery so rudely undone.

I've done some writing seminars for children. We talk

together about imagination. I always make them promise that they won't let theirs die as they grow up. Jesus would do the same, I think. Children are also readily teachable, trustful, and responsive.

When maturity comes to mean that all these wonderful qualities have long since dried up, we may be well on the way to becoming Pharisees or spiritual automatons. Instead, we must develop even further our childlike supple responsiveness, for it will enhance our fruitfulness more and more as we grow older and closer to His coming.

LIFE UNDER FIRE AND WITHOUT QUARTER

As we wait for Jesus' coming, we are not just called to maintain a lifestyle of preparedness. We also are to hold a wartime mentality. We are at war. Not only a war, but we are engaged in the greatest conflict in the history of the universe. In human conflict, there are truces or cease-fires, such as during World War I when German and Allied soldiers joined on Christmas Eve to sing carols together. But in the clash between the forces of the kingdom of God and the forces of the powers of darkness, there is never a truce or a cease-fire. No "quarter" (mercy toward an enemy) is given. There also are no conscientious objectors or noncombatants.

Scripture is plain here. The enemy is never just Pharaoh, the priests of Baal, Annas, Caiaphas, or Pontius Pilate. We face supernatural enemies who operate both on their own and through human instruments who are unknowing and willing. Exactly who are we dealing with? Satan is not some primitive attempt to incarnate an impersonal evil. His evil is in a living mind and personality. And he is our enemy, whether we believe in him or not. There is a genius to evil that is too systematic and beyond the intellect of evil's most proficient practitioners to be explained in human terms even by secular observers.

> A Scotland Yard Inspector was once asked if he believed in the devil. He replied like this: "Yes, I do, although I have never seen him. Sometimes in London there is an out reach of petty crime, and the quality of the criminals caught show that they are not intelligent enough to have planned the crime. So we know that there is a new leader, and we open a new file, 'Mr. X.' We then build up a picture of what he is, and from that we seek to find him. In the same way, as I cross-examine people on how they got into the mess they are in, I find there is a 'Mr. X' who is twisting our lives. That 'Mr. X' is the Devil."[3]

The military metaphors of the New Testament are too abundant and earnest to allow any serious reader the illusion that life for a Christian is a soft, tame thing (see 2 Corinthians 10:3-4; Ephesians 6:10-13; 1 Timothy 1:18, 6:12; 2 Timothy 2:3-4, 4:7).

When we hear of spiritual warfare, of what do we think? Probably we envision major things like spreading the gospel into unreached areas or casting out demons—blatant, larger-than-life events. Spiritual warfare certainly means all these dramatic things, but it is also something much closer to home. The basic things of everyday life—that's where the most intense fighting will take place. How we think and exercise our faith daily, the way we conduct our marriage and raise our children, how we perform on the job and relate to our fellow employees and the people in the neighborhood—here is where the fiercest combat will go on. These areas are the grass roots of society.

Christians striving to be faithful to Christ in these

things are truly being leaven and light to their culture, for it is in these areas that the kingdom of God penetrates society. The dark forces in this world don't want our marriages to work, our kids to turn out all right, or our faith to flourish. They are feverishly set against it. If Satan can spiritually neutralize us in these ways, he will not have to worry about how many demons we cast out. We ignore or take the mundane things of life for granted at our peril.

We dare not underestimate our enemy. True, the Bible describes Satan as a defeated foe (Colossians 2:15). But it is a mixture of ignorance, pride, and presumption to be almost flippant, the way some Christians are, about writing him off. Scripture also says he is no one to toy with or turn our backs on: "Be of sober spirit, be on the alert. Your adversary, the devil, prowls about like a roaring lion, seeking someone to devour" (1 Peter 5:8).

The depth of Satan's wickedness and malice is impossible for us to conceive. His might is powerful beyond imagination. We are no match. Only Christ is stronger. That's why we should cling to the Bible's admonition to put on Christ and be strong in His might.

We are the Evil One's targets. Satan hates the kingdom of God. He has his *own* kingdom he's constantly trying to expand. He refuses to admit defeat unless he's brought directly under the constraint of the Cross. This is nothing less than the same virulent pride that made him aspire to be like God and engineered his fall in the first place.

Satan hates Christians. Because of Christ, believers will rule with Christ and will judge angels. In eternity we will be conformed to Christ's image. In this life we can exercise Christ's authority over Satan. The one who desired to make himself like God will be forced to bow his knee to the same pathetic little creatures he tormented for thousands of years on earth. It will be a righteous humiliation as only the Son of God can forge it. Satan regards us with unearthly venom.

I don't write this to make anyone look under his bed or check his closet before turning out the light. There are times when not to be scared is the sure badge of madness or stupidity. We should be scared—scared enough to strap on our spiritual armor good and tight (Ephesians 6:13-18). Jesus Himself warns us against becoming so intoxicated with spiritual victory that we become conceited and downright cocky over victories won in Christ's strength as if they'd been won in our own (Luke 10:17-20). Underestimating the strength and venom of our enemy is the first step toward that empty pride. People who do are strong candidates to end up with his tread marks on their face. And not all get up again.

Satan's deepest hatred is reserved for God, the One he wanted to usurp as ruler over heaven and the One who engineered his ultimate defeat through Christ. He cannot hurt God directly. Scars from an angelic war before time remind him of defeat and exile from heaven along with one third of all angels. But Satan takes a malevolent delight in knowing that as he hurts God's children he wounds God as well. Many of us fail to think much about this. If flawed human parents deeply feel the pain of their children, how much more does a perfect heavenly Father with unfailing love feel vicariously the pain from Satan's lashing of His children, who were adopted at the price of the blood of His Son?

In a Sunday school class one morning the subject of seat belts came up. Someone made the statement that seat belts didn't make any difference. He said he resented the laws requiring their use. One young woman, a paramedic, spoke up. She said, "Down at work we have a name for people who don't wear seat belts. We call them organ donors."

There's also a name for those who ignore Satan, underestimate his strength and intent, and are blithely unaware that their whole life is the backdrop for combat of the fiercest, most insidious kind. They're called spiritual fatalities.

Knowing these fearful truths, we must not run and hide. Those who seek the kingdom of God are called to the attack. David Livingstone, the well-known missionary to Africa, said, "I am prepared to go anywhere, provided it is forward." Too many have a passive spiritual mindset that views Christianity as remedial. They think one should keep it on hand like something in the medicine cabinet for those times when the soul needs a Band-Aid or an aspirin. We all need to have our minds opened to the reality of the warfare. We now belong to an army spanning centuries, an army that means to advance Christ's kingdom against all foes. It is our challenge to see a traditionally misinterpreted Scripture with new eyes: "You are Peter, and upon this rock I will build My church; and the gates of Hades shall not overpower it" (Matthew 16:18).

We usually envision the church safely ensconced within massive stone walls. From high on the wall Christians peer down sticking their tongues out at a handful of scruffy demons who are holding a battering ram outside. That isn't what Matthew 16:18 says at all. The gates are not the gates of the church but of hell. In our mind's eye have we ever seen them? They must be massive and thick. They're inlaid with all the transitory material baubles people strive to attain in this life. It's more than just ironic that these people drool, crawl, and even sell their own souls to enter through those doors where they will perish.

I see these people everywhere—in my church, in counseling, at the mall, on the news. In my heart I have seen enough of these hellish gates to be sick of them, to viscerally hate them. But God has commissioned a certain group of people to destroy those gates. These are the ones who follow Christ, the pursuers of the kingdom of God. These assailants of hell will not be content with a *laissez faire* approach with Satan (you leave me alone and I'll leave you alone). Christians should not be on the defensive in the spiritual battle. God has called us to put on the spiritual armor and then to stand and fight (Ephesians 6).

> When the Spartans marched into battle, they advanced with cheerful songs, willing to fight. But when the Persians entered the conflict, you could hear as the regiments came on the crack of whips by which the officers drove the cowards into the thick of the battle. You need not wonder that a few Spartans were more than a match for thousands of Persians, that in fact they were like lions in the midst of sheep.
>
> So let it be with the church; never should she need to be forced to reluctant action. Full of irrepressible life, she should long for conflict against everything which is contrary to God.
>
> Were we enthusiastic soldiers of the cross, we should be like lions in the midst of herds of enemies, and through God's help nothing would be able to stand against us.[4]

In order to have the right frame of mind for spiritual battle, we must remember our own resurrection character. Like our Lord, the people seeking His kingdom have a remarkable way of rising again. Often the church's greatest moments have come at the very brink of extinction. The resurrection of Jesus is the greatest example. Everything seemed totally destroyed until the third day. Then came the victory.

Persecution seemed to be the way to get rid of those early Christians, but as the Romans watched the way those early believers died, they became convinced of a higher truth behind their commitment. Probably nothing else could have accomplished such a deep impression. The same phenomenon could be traced through the Reformation, the great awakenings, and the outstanding nineteenth century of missionary outreach where every volunteer's death spurred half a dozen to take his place.

We do not fight for Christ in His strength against Satanic hordes. We fight *with* Him, for the battle is His, not ours. The kingdom of God's success is never tied to our own. Since Christ saved us and set us on the road to seek His kingdom, we are to be about His business until He returns.

Our calling is to do what our Lord says to do—with all our hearts. Although demons hang leering over this dying world like gargoyles, we in the kingdom of God should neither be swayed nor intimidated by them. We'll not need to look far to do battle with the principalities and powers. If we set our hearts on Christ's kingdom above all, they will surely find us. It is for us to live with commitment, so that they *do* find us. Then, when they do, we fight for Christ in His strength, putting the forces of darkness to flight.

NEW TREASURE TO BE PLACED IN OUR HANDS

As we look into the future seeking God's kingdom, we should live with the certain hope that when Christ returns, culminating the establishment of His kingdom, He will bring His reward with Him (1 Corinthians 3:14, 2 Timothy 4:8, 1 Peter 5:4, Revelation 22:12). We get an idea of what is involved in our reward in the letters to the seven churches in Revelation. The format is the same for each letter. A portrayal of some aspect of the opening vision of Christ is followed by a critique of the church, listing both strengths and weaknesses. Then comes an admonition to pay heed to what was said ("He who has an ear"). Finally, each of the seven letters closes with the promise of a certain reward to those who overcome.

Overcoming was an important theme to John. Between the Gospel of John, the Johannine Epistles, and Revelation, the word *overcome* appears seventeen times. The Christians he wrote for weren't super Christians who never failed. These were people who struggled, failed, fought back again and again, and knew that their final victory was not to be had on this planet. Neither was their reward. Let's take a look at the seven rewards in Revelation 2 and 3.

The first reward promised is a choice one: "To him who overcomes, I will grant to eat of the tree of life, which is in the Paradise of God" (Revelation 2:7). Certainly this does not mean just literal fruit. Some see it as a restoration of what was lost in Eden. Access to the "life" tree will be given as a reward. This is a tree whose fruit gives life as only Jesus could promise or give (John 10:10). While that is true even now, it will be true in eternity in ways far beyond what we experience today.

Paul says that in the next life the perishable must put on the imperishable (1 Corinthians 15:53). It will be a life that goes beyond restoring what was lost in Adam's fall, a life in a new body that will demonstrate capacities we now would regard as supernatural. Pain, sickness, and aging will be unknown. Since they are now only signposts in a fallen world to keep us moving toward eternity, we'll no longer need them. A quality of life that is unimaginable now will fit us like a tailored glove.

J. Robertson McQuilkin, president of Columbia Bible College, was once approached by an elderly lady facing these trials. "Robertson, why does God let us get old and weak? Why must I hurt so?" she asked him.

After a few moments thought he replied, "I think God has planned the strength and beauty of youth to be physical. But the strength and beauty of age is spiritual. We gradually lose the strength and beauty that is temporary so we'll be sure to concentrate on the strength and beauty which is forever. And so we'll be eager to leave the temporary, deteriorating part of us and be truly homesick for our eternal home. If we stayed young and strong and beautiful, we might never want to leave!"[5]

Second, Jesus said, "He who overcomes shall not be hurt by the second death" (Revelation 2:11). The second death is the lake of fire pictured in Revelation 20:14-15. Judgment is the great omega point of the human race. It is inescapable: "It is appointed for men to die once and after this comes judgment" (Hebrews 9:27). But the Christian has nothing to fear in that day.

It is true that the Christian can be confident that God will not scrap him at death. It is true he can rest with assurance on this promise of Jesus. He can look forward to death not as the end, but as the end of the caterpillar stage. . . . We may choose whether when we die we rot, or whether death becomes for us the chrysalis case to usher in a new quality of life with the Risen One.[6]

A third reward for believers is hidden manna and a white stone with a new name written on it, which no one knows but the one who receives it (Revelation 2:17). Alluding to the physical food called manna that was provided for the children of Israel under Moses, hidden manna refers to spiritual feeding and nourishment (as in living water or the bread of life). Hidden refers not to being hard to find but obscure, because it's being reserved for those whose hearts are specially prepared. In heaven, those who overcome will not only understand whole vistas of God's truth that were cloudy in this life, but that truth will nourish us beyond anything we can imagine.

Some think that the white stone will hold a new name for Christ. But I agree with those who think the new name will be for *us*. Despite all the multitudes who will be in heaven, we will still be known as individuals, by special names given to us by God. Each of us will have intimacies with Him known and treasured all to ourselves. Quality time with His children won't be a problem. He'll have all eternity with us.

A fourth reward is that those who overcome will also receive authority to rule the nations with a rod of iron and will receive the morning star (Revelation 2:26-28). The first of these promises states that the people of the heavenly kingdom will share Christ's rule and will reign with Him (Matthew 19:28; Luke 22:29-30; 1 Corinthians 6:2; Revelation 12:5, 19:15).

How many of us know anything at all about ruling nations, or have any desire to do so? In college I served on the board of directors of the college foundation. Suddenly I was plunged into a world of financial statements, legal briefs, and detailed documents that might as well have been written in Sanskrit. The vice president took me under his wing, letting me know of his confidence that I would grow into what I needed to know and do.

On a cosmic level, Jesus Christ will do even more than that to enable us. Besides, we'll not serve in this way because we worked ourselves into the job; it will be an eternal reminder of His grace.

The gift of the morning star is Jesus Himself (Revelation 22:16). Who could desire a reward any greater than Christ? We could stop here and say no more, but the rewards go on.

The fifth set of rewards includes white garments and our names preserved in the book of life (Revelation 3:5). Christ Himself will confess our names before the Father and His angels. The redeemed will wear white robes, which will eternally call us to live for Christ's glory, for the honor symbolized by the garment. Our names will be indelibly inscribed on the registry in heaven. Jesus Himself will preserve our identity as citizens of heaven. We will forever be citizens of the kingdom we sought.

Moreover, Christ Himself will stand before the Father and angels to confess that you and I are His. On my left hand is my third wedding band—but still my first marriage. I've accidentally lost two wedding bands, and with the loss of the second, my wife determinedly decided the next one would not come off for anything. She wanted people to know that I was hers. The sheer glee and joy with which Christ will shout to the galaxies that I am home and that I am His is unfathomable. It will be just as joyful for us all.

Sixth, we see that we who overcome are promised that we will become pillars in the Temple of God, and that we'll be engraved with a three-fold name (Revelation 3:12). Pillars endure. They are a symbol of permanence and durability, if the ruins of Greece and Rome have anything to teach us. The people who first heard these words would understand right away since they lived in a region notorious for severe earthquakes.

Today we should understand as well. Who among us hasn't seen resolve and good intentions blow away like sand in the wind? Have you ever tried to be strong, only to collapse like a house of cards at temptation in an offguard moment? The days of being so collapsible will end in eternity. Then our obedience will not be sporadic, our desire to please God no longer frustrated by our sin. The new life we'll enjoy there will be bedrock stuff.

The three-fold name of God, the new Jerusalem, and Christ's new name underscore themes already mentioned. Having God's name written on us underscores intimate possession—not mere ownership but cherishing what is owned: "You were sealed in Him with the Holy Spirit of promise . . . with a view to the redemption of God's own possession, to the praise of His glory" (Ephesians 1:13-14).

The name "new Jerusalem" underscores our citizenship, and Christ's new name underscores His personal relationship with us. Jesus wants to let us know that His Father really cherishes us. Can adopted children ever have too much reassurance of their Father's love? This was especially true for the churches receiving these letters, for they were heading into the buzz saw of Roman persecution. What a contrast between this verse and the cosmic nothingness and extinction of self that is touted as nirvana, the ultimate goal of Eastern mysticism that is being lapped up by millions today under New Age guise!

Finally, we are promised that we will sit with Christ on His very throne: "He who overcomes, I will grant to him to sit down with Me on My throne, as I also overcame and sat down with My Father on His throne" (Revelation 3:21).

This is almost too much. It would be blasphemous if it weren't true. While the picture of sitting on God's throne underscores our ruling with Him, it also serves as an eternal reminder of something else. We have gained all these eternal privileges and treasures, not because *we* overcame but because *Jesus* overcame. The Lamb slain before the foundation of the world threw off glory like a cape of light to enter obscurely into a dying humanity. The odds were stacked against Him. Nevertheless, He overcame. The only reason anyone else can overcome at all is because the Son of God went first. It's just like the Son of Man (the name He most often chose for Himself—because it identifies with us) to link Himself to us, even on His throne. Across time and space Christ calls to us as we take our turn at the battle to advance His kingdom. As He calls, He promises as only He can that a very special seat is being saved—a promise from one overcomer to another.

PRESSING INTO THE FUTURE

Two old gentlemen of the theater stepped out into the evening after an enthralling few hours with the Chicago Symphony. The program had been superb and varied. But the finale of a Beethoven symphony brought down the house with thunderous applause and sent the crowds buzzing into the night.

Heads down, the two men were caught between animated conversation and reverential awe at what they'd heard. One had been speaking and had walked almost a hundred feet before he realized he was alone. Turning around he was amazed at what he saw. His friend had stopped to listen to a young poorly-dressed man, sitting with his hat on the sidewalk in front of him. It wasn't uncommon for street musicians to set up shop where people were exiting theaters, where they might pick up some change or even a few bills from passersby.

As the one gentleman came back to join his friend, he heard the whine and plaintive sound of the young man's harmonica. Not until he got close did he recognize the tune. It was a short version of the Beethoven finale they had just heard. At its conclusion, the first man who had stopped to listen slowly raised his hands and applauded with the same dignity and respect he would have given the conductor of the Chicago Symphony. Then he reached into his billfold and extracted a fifty dollar bill. He placed it in the hat and turned to leave.

His friend could contain his astonishment no longer. "How could you do that?" he said. "How could you listen to the incredible performance we heard tonight and then give a gift like that to some street hack who dared to play on his pitiful harmonica the same themes we heard?"

The first man gave a self-assured grin and said, with a hint of awe hanging in his voice, "It was still Beethoven."

Jesus Christ, who has never broken His word, promised that He would return. Until He does, we live in between His comings, faced with the momentous decision as to how we will spend this one short life we have. We can spend it only once. We have looked at what the kingdom of God is, what it means to belong to it, what it costs to seek it, and finally, where it is going and how we should live in light of that sense of direction. Yet we've barely scratched the surface.

But one thing we can all know for sure is that the kingdom of God has room for lives of every shape and size. Both the sophisticated and the uncultivated must enter by way of the Cross. Regardless of the quality of human instrumentality, those who will set out from the Cross to seek and advance the kingdom of God will always find it is still Jesus Christ alone who brings music to lowly hearts, while most people are too busy dying in their inanely important ways to listen. It is a profound irony that only those who seek first and foremost the kingdom of God and its sublime music will find it.

Notes

CHAPTER 2

1. E. Stanley Jones, *The Unshakable Kingdom and the Unchanging Person* (Nashville: Abingdon Press, 1972), pages 263-264.
2. Michael Green, *You Must Be Joking: Popular Excuses for Avoiding Jesus Christ* (Wheaton, Ill.: Tyndale House Publishers, 1976), page 35.
3. Max Lucado, *No Wonder They Call Him Savior: Chronicles of the Cross* (Portland, Oreg.: Multnomah Press, 1986), page 73.

CHAPTER 3

1. Kenneth Scott Latourette, *A History of Christianity* (New York: Harper & Row, 1953), pages 1473-1474.
2. George Eldon Ladd, *Jesus and the Kingdom* (Grand Rapids: Eerdmans Publishing Co., 1964), pages 220-221.
3. A. Skevington Wood, *The Inextinguishable Blaze: Spiritual Renewal and Advance in the 18th Century* (Grand Rapids:

Eerdmans Publishing Co., 1960), page 188.

4. J. Oswald Sanders, *Spiritual Leadership* (Chicago: Moody Press, 1967), page 113.

5. J.I. Packer, *Knowing God* (Downers Grove, Ill.: Inter-Varsity Press, 1973), pages 95-96.

CHAPTER 5

1. William Barclay, *Gospel of Luke* (Philadelphia: Westminster Press, 1976), pages 285-286.

2. C.H. Spurgeon, quoted in *Closer Walk* (Colorado Springs, Colo.: The Navigators, February 1989), page 17.

3. E. Stanley Jones, *The Unshakable Kingdom*, page 54.

4. Frederick Buechner, *Wishful Thinking* (New York: Harper & Row, 1973), page 28.

CHAPTER 6

1. Frederick Buechner, *Wishful Thinking*, pages 67-69.

2. Garth Lean, *God's Politician* (Colorado Springs, Colo.: Helmers and Howard Publishers, 1987), page 43.

3. Robert Fulgham, *All I Really Need to Know I Learned in Kindergarten* (New York: Villard Books, 1988), pages 189-191.

4. E. Stanley Jones, *The Unshakable Kingdom*, page 42.

5. Richard F. Lovelace, *Dynamics of Spiritual Life: An Evangelical Theology of Renewal* (Downers Grove, Ill.: Inter-Varsity Press, 1979), page 88.

6. Calvin Miller, *The Singer* (Downers Grove, Ill.: Inter-Varsity Press, 1975), pages 102-103.

7. Walter Hollenweger, *Evangelism Today*, Christian Journals Ltd., page 7, as quoted in David Watson, *I Believe in the Church* (Grand Rapids: Eerdmans Publishing Co., 1978), pages 301-302.

8. Eugene Peterson, *Run with the Horses* (Downers Grove, Ill.: InterVarsity Press, 1983), page 50.

9. David Watson, *I Believe in Evangelism* (Grand Rapids: Eerdmans Publishing Co., 1976), pages 52-53.

10. John Pollock, *Victims of the Long March* (Waco, Tex.: Word, Inc., 1970), page 55.

CHAPTER 7

1. Richard Collier, *The General Next to God* (London: Collins, 1965), page 103.

2. Calvin Miller, *The Singer*, pages 124-125.

3. Amy Carmichael, quoted in J. Oswald Sanders, *Spiritual Leadership* (Chicago: Moody Press, 1967), page 45.

4. Oswald Chambers, *My Utmost for His Highest* (New York: Dodd, Mead and Co., 1935), page 271.

5. J.I. Packer, *Knowing God*, page 227.

6. Frederick Buechner, *Wishful Thinking*, page 2.

7. Ruth Bell Graham, *Legacy of a Pack Rat* (Nashville: Thomas Nelson Publishers, 1989), pages 44-48.

8. R.V.G. Tasker, *The Gospel According to St. Matthew: Tyndale New Testament Commentaries* (Grand Rapids: Eerdmans Publishing Co., 1975), page 62.

9. Francis A. Schaeffer, *The Church at the End of the Twentieth Century* (Downers Grove, Ill.: InterVarsity Press, 1970), page 144.

10. John R.W. Stott, *Christian Counter-Culture: The Message of the Sermon on the Mount* (Downers Grove, Ill.: InterVarsity Press, 1978), page 51.

11. Martha Skelton, "Northern Ireland: Many Barriers, Few Bridges," *The Commission* (May 1989), page 25.

12. Donald Bloesch, *Crumbling Foundations: Death and Rebirth in an Age of Upheaval* (Grand Rapids: Zondervan Publishing House, 1984), page 98.

13. Philip Yancey, *Where Is God When It Hurts?* (Grand Rapids: Zondervan Publishing House, 1977), page 15.

CHAPTER 8

1. J.I. Packer, *Knowing God*, page 182.
2. Carl F.H. Henry, *God, Revelation and Authority, Vol. II: God Who Speaks and Shows* (Waco, Tex.: Word, Inc., 1976), page 173.
3. Leon Morris, *I Believe in Revelation* (Grand Rapids: Eerdmans Publishing Co., 1976), page 42.
4. Richard Collier, *The General Next to God*, pages 237-238.

CHAPTER 9

1. J.I. Packer, *Knowing God*, page 56.
2. David Watson, *I Believe in Evangelism*, page 100.
3. Helen S. Shoemaker, *I Stand by the Door* (New York: Harper & Row, 1967), pages ix-x.

CHAPTER 10

1. David Watson, *I Believe in Evangelism*, pages 12-13.
2. Ron R. Lee, "Whatever Happened to the American Dream?" *Marriage Partnership* (Spring 1988), page 42.
3. Paul L. Wachtel, *The Poverty of Affluence—A Psychological Analysis of Life in a Consumer Society* (Free Press of America, 1983), page 17.
4. David B. Barrett, "Annual Statistical Table on Global Mission: 1988," *International Bulletin of Missionary Research*, Vol. 12, No. 1 (January 1988), pages 16-17.
5. J.I. Packer, *Knowing God*, page 21.
6. Marty Croll, "When Volunteers Come Back: A Change in Values," *The Commission* (June/July 1988), pages 56-58.

CHAPTER 11

1. Mike Yaconelli, "Becoming Pagan," *The Wittenburg Door*, Nos. 98, 99 (August-November 1987), pages 61-64.
2. John E. Cooke, *Stonewall Jackson: A Military Biography* (New York: D. Appleton and Company, 1876), page 248.
3. Iain Murray, *D. Martyn-Lloyd Jones: The First Forty Years, 1899-1939* (Carlisle, Penn.: The Banner of Truth Trust, 1982), pages 263-264.

CHAPTER 12

1. Ray Stedman, *The Ruler Who Serves: Mark 8-16* (Waco, Tex.: Word, Inc., 1976), page 66.
2. Ray Stedman, *The Ruler Who Serves*, page 67.
3. David Watson, *I Believe in Evangelism*, page 149.
4. Charles H. Spurgeon, quoted in *Closer Walk* (June 1989), page 23.
5. Philip Yancey, *Where Is God . . . ?*, page 155.
6. Michael Green, *You Must Be Joking*, page 183.

FOR A FREE CATALOG OF
NAVPRESS BOOKS & BIBLE STUDIES,
CALL TOLL FREE 800-366-7788 (USA)
or 1-416-499-4615 (CANADA)